critical praise

"*Am I Doing This Right?* is the comprehensive personal story of one woman's grieving following the death of her husband. It is written in an engaging and straightforward style that traces her experiences from diagnosis, early caregiving, admission to hospice, his death, subsequent memorials, and the years following. One notable feature is the author's awareness of the subtle but continued impacts of grief even five years after his death. She is strong enough to be candid about her mistakes and the disappointments she feels in herself and others. Linda presents herself as an example but not a model for grieving. She doesn't presume to give advice or write a to-do list for her readers. *Am I Doing This Right?* is an articulate, self-revealing, and very readable account of one woman's journey after the death of her spouse, but it would be an excellent resource for anyone facing the loss of a loved one."
— **Paul K. Fehrenbach**, PhD, retired clinical psychologist, hospice and bereavement volunteer

"A marvelous, honest account of grief with all the seemingly bizarre mysteries, contradictions, epiphanies, and comfort in life after loss. I love the simple clarity and honesty, as well as the sense of story. Something everyone experiencing grief should read. I learned so much from reading it, and I'm sure others will be grateful Patterson took the time to write it."
— **Marlene Jones**, retired International Coaching Federation certified life coach

"As the author states, 'everyone's route through grief is unique to them.' She has written an unflinchingly honest and compassionate account of her own, which readers will find relevant and encouraging. The author's compelling prose exceeds its goal of honoring all others' grief journeys. It is a privilege to recommend *Am I Doing This Right?* and, yes Ms. Patterson, you are."

- **Ann Ritter**, MA, ThM, retired chaplain and
bereavement counselor, UNC Hospice

"After the death of her beloved husband, Linda pulls her broken pieces back together and finds her 'new normal.' Many have pondered the question of whether there actually is 'life' after death, and Linda proves it without a doubt. Once I started reading, I couldn't put it down."

– **Tami Boardman**, end-of-life doula

"Comprehensive, heart-wrenching, and reflective describe Linda Patterson's account of living through the last days of her husband's life and the first years of widowhood. With no roadmap, and not sure how to negotiate the future, Patterson makes her way down dead ends, rocky roads, and wrong turns to emerge a stronger and healthier, independent woman. Not only widows, but all of us will take meaning and comfort from this book."

– **Karen L. Shectman**, PhD in family and
child development, retired chaplain

am i doing this right?

finding my way through grief

Linda Patterson

LYSTRA BOOKS
& Literary Services

Am I Doing This Right? Finding My Way Through Grief
Copyright © 2022 Linda Patterson

ISBN paperback 979-8-9850083-0-2
ISBN ebook 979-8-9850083-1-9
Library of Congress Control Number: 2021925578

Author's photo by Linda Patterson

Book design by Kelly Prelipp Lojk

Published by Lystra Books & Literary Services, LLC
391 Lystra Estates Drive
Chapel Hill, NC 27517
lystrabooks@gmail.com

This book is dedicated to
my late husband, John Clinton Watts,
and my children Henry Andrew Watterson
and Grace Ryung Watterson.

Author's Note: I have told this story to the best of my recollection despite the fog of grief and the twists and turns of memory. However, most of my memories are backed up by diary notes, my calendar, and my children. If you were there, you may have had a different perspective. I have tried to recreate dialog from memory to bring the scenes alive. Some names have been changed, but I have used real family names. Reliving the details of John's illness, death, and my early widowhood has been a very healing process.

foreword

Is there any way to do death right? From the moment my husband was diagnosed with his rare, aggressive bile duct cancer, I did the best job I could to support him. When he died, I bravely carried on.

I kept my feelings in check and maintained a frenzied pace of volunteer work, village activities, lunches with friends, and bereavement groups to ward off despair.

I appeared to be doing very well. But what about my interior life? Was I really doing this right?

As each year passed, I became fascinated that it was different from the year before. How many iterations of grief could there be? As I looked back, I could admit that my first year was characterized by denial. I cried most days the second year after John's death, so I think of it as the year of sadness. All the denial of my emotions the first year probably reappeared as health issues in my third year of bereavement, but the fourth year brought me some relief as I started to integrate everything I had learned from the challenging first three years.

If I were to pick up a pencil and draw my journey, I would start with a question mark. Then the line would plunge, go in one direction and another, dip low, bump along, pitch up and down, and finally spiral toward its center, where it would come to rest.

I present the story of my grief to honor all others. Everyone who grieves takes his or her own path. No one else can follow another's footsteps. Each of us is unique and each of our relationships is unique. Your grief is like no other. And, yes, I am doing this right, right for me.

this is a test

I felt like I was being tested. The DVD player failed, the network extender no longer worked so I couldn't make phone calls from home, my computer monitor fizzled, and my husband's car battery died. The electric toothbrush wouldn't activate, and the microwave stopped heating food. I couldn't turn on all three lamps in the living room without blowing a fuse. My husband John had died a few months before. I had to cope with all these situations alone, without his suggestions or wise counsel. He had been our family tech guru. I reassured myself I could handle these challenges even without his valuable half of our partnership brain.

I spent more than ten hours searching Internet help pages and on the phone with technical support reps trying to sort out my telephone woes. Finally, I found a rep who understood my problem and suggested I buy a new cell phone that used Wi-Fi calling. Then I wouldn't need a network extender.

I started using John's old monitor instead of buying a new one.

I hired an electrician to fix the living room fuse.

I had the car battery replaced and, while in the car dealership, solicited a bid from them to buy the car.

I bought a new DVD player, electric toothbrush, and microwave. John and I never bought anything without doing a lot of research, so I read product reviews and solicited opinions from friends and neighbors.

As I worked through each of these challenges, my confidence grew.

After John's death, I was determined not to get depressed. Yes, I was sad and emotionally raw, but I didn't dwell on how much I would miss my husband's wit and intelligence or how much joy and satisfaction I received from my marriage. I concentrated on my future. Where was I going to live? Was I going to have enough money? What did I want to do with my time? How was I going to keep busy—busy enough to distract myself from the pain that was buried deep beneath my determination?

Eventually, the memories of what I once possessed started to filter into my consciousness. One of the first things I missed was the music in our household. John and I both loved musical theater; a single word could remind us of a song and set us singing. When our son Henry was three, he stood at the top of his grandmother's basement stairs, offered her his tiny hand, and sang, "Take my hand, I'm a stranger in paradise." My mother laughed and said, "Where did you learn that?" Henry said, "Mommy and Daddy always sing that before we go downstairs." One year at a large Thanksgiving celebration,

Henry, aged five, wandered from table to table singing the entire score of *The Music Man*. Another time, before driving off to see the Disney movie *Beauty and the Beast*, our family stood in the kitchen and sang songs from the show. Grace, three years younger than Henry, was also very musical, but not as much of a ham as the rest of us. It seemed that someone in our household was always in rehearsals for a musical or theater production.

John loved being silly or "goofy," as his children described him. He mimicked Bullwinkle and collected small stuffed characters from the cartoon show. He adored comedy and did the Monty Python silly walks in public. He loved Pogo cartoons and had a collection of Pogo cups, records, shirts, books, and other memorabilia. He could get lost in laughing.

Music and humor were just two things that bound us together. Another was household renovation projects. John grew up without a father present, but he could do carpentry, plumbing, electrical work, and landscaping, all self-taught. I grew up with a father who had a wood shop, built furniture, and had high standards for painting walls and woodwork. Together, John and I could tackle most home projects. Our first house was a ten-room post-Victorian that needed a lot of work. I sanded and refinished almost all the floors. The first story had solid oak floors, but the second and third stories had beautiful bird's-eye maple floors. Four coats of polyurethane made these floors gleam.

John removed and rearranged the cabinetry in the kitchen, and then we laid the counter with colorful Mexican tile. John even plumbed in a bright blue ceramic sink. Seven years later, in our next house, we hired someone to renovate the kitchen, but we tiled the kitchen countertop. We also laid a brick walkway and patios in the front and back. We slowed down as we aged, but there was always a project to do, and we loved it.

I loved John's intellect too. We both had our strengths in this regard, but he was an avid reader and kept up with news and politics. When he attended lectures, he always had questions for the speakers. He read extensively on the Internet and supported many nonprofit organizations that protected the environment or presented in-depth research on the federal budget or the US Department of Defense spending. I was not particularly interested in politics or the news before I married John, but I consider it a gift that his interest sparked mine.

I could go on and on about how compatible John and I were, how much fun we had on trips to Africa and Korea and to Canada for dog-sledding. How we had similar taste and enjoyed the same kinds of foods. How we almost never fought. How we both loved animals, especially cats. In fact, when we were young, we each had a cat named Henry. We had a happy, compatible married life that was full of riches, until the source of the treasure was gone.

glimpses of the future

John walked into the kitchen, absent-mindedly tugging at his khakis.

I said, "Why do you keep hiking up your pants?"

"I must have lost weight," he said, looking down at his belt. He didn't have much weight to spare, considering he was 5'11" and weighed 140 pounds. His thirty-two-inch-waist pants hung low on his hips.

"We should buy you some new pants before we go to California at Christmas," I said.

"Hmmm. I'll make an appointment to see my doctor when we get back."

John was not one to go to the doctor often. When he said he would make the appointment, it hit me at a visceral level. As I stood there paring potatoes, a warm flush started in my chest and spread over my neck and face. I recalled the words of my primary care doctor years ago. "When you start losing weight, it's too late." I never forgot her warning because I was hypervigilant about my health, bordering on hypochondria.

I feared that I was on a path to losing John.

In late December 2015, John and I flew to San Francisco, where we met our twenty-seven-year-old daughter, Grace, who had flown in from Boston. She told me later that when she first greeted her dad, she noticed how thin he looked. I hadn't noticed because I saw him every day.

We rented a car and drove to our son Henry's apartment. We parked the car on the hill in front of his apartment and hiked up the steep steps to his front door. He and his partner lived in a typical San Francisco brownstone with a giant front window that looked like it had never been washed. We listened to Henry play his newly acquired accordion, bought on a lark in a thrift store. Grace and John took turns trying it out before we left to spend a few days in Davis before Christmas with John's cousin Faye and her adult daughter Amber. We had a wonderful time riding bikes around Davis and visiting their homes, but before we left, I picked up a stomach bug and passed it on to John.

On the next leg of our trip, John and I retreated to the back seat of the car, where he lay with his head on my lap. Henry navigated while Grace drove us over the beautiful California hills towards the coast, where we had rented a house in Mendocino. The open-layout cottage was nestled in the woods and had a wooden outdoor hot tub that Henry and Grace enjoyed one evening. We spent our days driving along the California coast, stepping in and out of shops in the villages, walking the shoreline, and playing board games at night. On Christmas eve, John was still under the weather, so Henry, Grace, and I went to an upscale vegan restaurant in a nice hotel for dinner.

A couple of days later, we returned to the hotel so John could see where we had eaten. In the gift shop, he tried on a variety of hats and bought a fedora, something he had wanted for a while. Now when I look at pictures of him in that hat, I wonder why I encouraged him to buy it. I suspected he would not be living a long life, but if he wanted the hat, I wanted him to have it. It was a good-looking hat on a good-looking guy, but it was from another era. These days, fedoras seem like affectations, and John never put on airs.

After he died, I couldn't part with the hat and kept it perched on the base of an unfinished clay lamp I had made. He owned the hat briefly and wore it even less. Nevertheless, it held a memory of a more vibrant time, a time when John was in his beloved California where he went to college, and where we enjoyed our last Christmas together.

I left the hat displayed for a year, even though I gave away most of his clothes quickly in the days that followed his death. Eventually I was able to part with his hat too. But it took time.

changing landscape

I worked as a freelance video producer at the local public television station and loved every minute. On January 1, 2016, the show I contributed to was cut from five days to one day a week, and the station decided to only use their in-house staff. I was out of a job, but John's visit to his doctor changed that. Caring for John turned out to be my next project.

John's doctor felt an enlarged liver under his ribs and ordered imaging. He suspected cancer. It took over a week for the hospital staff to call and set the ultrasound appointment. I couldn't sit still while we waited.

"Have they called yet? Have you called them? What do mean you don't know who to call? I always ask for the number in case they don't call!"

I didn't want to nag at this tender time, but why didn't he push? Weight loss and an enlarged liver? This was scary. I wanted to find out what was going on. Maybe he didn't.

After John's initial appointment with his primary care doctor, John called Grace and said that his doctor thought he had cancer and needed tests. In a couple more weeks, he called again to say it definitely was cancer and it wasn't looking good.

He also talked to Henry, his mother, his sister, and his cousins, including relatives on his father's side whom he had only met a few times. His parents had divorced when he was three, and he had had little contact with his father's side of the family.

I was amazed that he was so open with his extended family. Didn't he want to have a better handle on all this information before he opened up to people? He was showing his underbelly. I wouldn't have told anyone until I knew all the details of my condition and wrapped myself in armor.

Soon after John's diagnosis of bile duct cancer at the end of January, his intermittent back pain made him unable or unwilling to drive to appointments. Perhaps he wanted my support and to be taken care of. I didn't ask. In fact, I didn't think about it. After all, we used to tell our children, "We're a team." I was more than happy to drive him to his doctor visits. He may have only wanted my company, but he also got a good note taker and strong advocate. I asked questions, made appointments, and put notes in binders. I wanted to be part of the process, to feel connected to him, and in control of this unreal part of our lives. I wanted to know what his doctors were saying about his illness and what this meant for us. I was on high alert. This illness wasn't just happening to him, it was happening to both of us.

I am good at tackling projects, coordinating the various parts, and orchestrating successful conclusions. Being busy keeps me upbeat. There's a rhythm to managing appointments, chores, and meetings that I find energizing. It also keeps my mind occupied so I don't wander into the emotional realm. My dad's advice after a boyfriend broke up with me in high school was to keep busy, to distract myself. In fact, my family's style was to avoid emotional drama. Humor was fine, being upset was not. I learned this lesson well and find that distraction is a useful tool. If my mind wants to churn at night, I numb myself to sleep by listening to a television documentary or an audiobook read by an actor with a soothing voice. John's care was my next project.

John was as organized as I am. He set up an email list and updated his extended family as soon as he received new information. The subject line of his first email was "Status," but that eventually turned into a series of numbered emails. He sent his eighth status report right after he entered hospice care six months later. His communiqués were factual and detailed, never sentimental.

John remained communicative with his family, all scattered at a safe distance across the country. However, he maintained his usual reserve and privacy with people who knew him in our village. His family communication may have stemmed from his zeal for documentation. He was passionate about documenting his work as a computer programmer and our home renovation projects. When he worked on a big home project, he took before and in-progress photos to document it. His status emails were chronicling his illness and treatments for his family. This was the side of communication he liked—conveying facts—not expressing his feelings and sharing his thoughts. I used to chide him about not calling his mother very often. I was disappointed that our son didn't call us very often either, but it made sense that he was following his father's example.

We all processed John's diagnosis differently. He was an intellectual guy who spent hours on the Internet, researching the details and location of his tumor. Grace dealt with the uncertainty in much the same way. At one point, she asked me what stage cancer John had.

"I don't know. The doctor never said. It doesn't seem to matter what label it has. His cancer has metastasized to his backbone and lungs and I know that is bad," I said, surprised that I didn't know which of these common labels my husband had been assigned. He had been given a year to live by his oncologist. That's all I really needed to know.

I didn't know what the next year would hold, but I knew I would eventually be living on my own. The emotional part of that was too painful to contemplate, so I kept my mind busy with more concrete thoughts. Should I sell the house after John died? Should I stay in our village? Should I move back to Boston, where we had lived four years ago? Whether I was fixing up the house to sell or fixing it up to stay, I knew I wanted to clean up the yard. With the energy that comes from a new commitment, I ripped out bushes in the front yard and hauled bricks stacked in the back yard to the Habitat ReStore thrift store. I pulled things we had saved "just in case" out of the crawl space and drove them along with wooden lattice, tomato stakes, and old tires to the disposal station. There's something about cleaning out and organizing that lifts my spirits. I needed to feel in control for as long as I could, because my life would soon begin to wobble.

When Grace and Henry visited in the spring, John and I stood in our backyard, watching, as our son moved our woodpile to a less visible part of the yard, something we had meant to do for years. Henry seemed supercharged as he moved the logs from one spot to another. He had never enjoyed physical labor or family projects, but this was a way he could help. We appreciated his efforts.

There is nothing like a deadline to motivate people, but this deadline only existed in my head. Everything could have stayed the same, but I wanted to be ready. Ready for change. Moving or staying, without John, it was change. I was bracing myself.

In the first month of John's illness, I was able to maintain my usual roster of activities. My calendar was dotted with dates to read to Head Start classes, visit foster children, attend lectures, and meet friends for lunch. In mid-February, the beat changed. John's appointments for radiation, chemotherapy infusions, scans, labs, and doctor visits started to squeeze out my activities. After a week of daily radiation visits and chemotherapy the following two weeks, John was so exhausted and sick with side effects that he rested for a couple of weeks. During this time, my nursing duties slowed, and I was able to resume my usual activities. Before I left on a late morning errand, I always said, "Do you want me to make you some lunch before I go?" He always declined, preferring to get up to putter in the kitchen in a semblance of normalcy.

Then the cycle started again: two weeks of chemotherapy, then three weeks of rest and scans. If need be, I canceled my personal plans at a moment's notice because he was my priority.

By April, the doctors decided to use new medications since the first protocol hadn't halted the cancer. In fact, he required more radiation to slow the cancer eating away his vertebrae. There was never any talk of stopping therapy. We were of the same mind: we would do anything it took to prolong his life.

I focused on the tasks at hand: driving John to appointments, taking notes, setting up more appointments. I needed to identify and buy food that John would eat (which eventually was only granola bars) and get used to eating alone when John abruptly left the dinner table because of nausea. It always started with a cough. Every time he coughed, I'd say, "You're going to be sick. You need to get to the bathroom. Go, go, go!" He always hesitated, then ran to the bathroom and retched. When he was back on our bed, I respected his wishes for no radio, no television, no cats, no conversation. I understood on some level how terrible he felt, but I felt shut out.

I am not a natural caregiver. I laugh when I think that I wanted to be a nurse as a small child. I am not warm and fuzzy and am somewhat self-absorbed. I needed some practical advice and emotional support. What did a sick person need? What did they want? There was a caregiver group in my village that I very much wanted to join but didn't dare. John did not want me to tell anyone about his illness. He had only confided in his family and our close friends Peg and Jim across the street. The secrecy left me frustrated and isolated, with few people to confide in. My world was crumbling as I watched this once-vibrant man fade. Eventually, I told my closest friends on lunch dates and swore them to secrecy. To my knowledge, they all respected my wishes.

When John was in the hospital for his chemo infusions, I would stay with him or sometimes wander the hospital for exercise. I saw a flyer for a caregivers' lunch in the cancer hospital's patient and family resource center. I was thrilled that I would be there on the right day and be able to attend. It was a drop-in group, so some people had been dealing with a loved one's cancer for years, and others, like me, were new to the challenges of caregiving. I walked into a sunny conference room and was overwhelmed to see eleven people around the table—three professionals and eight caregivers. When it was my turn to introduce myself, my voice cracked, and tears rolled down my cheeks as I expressed my gratitude for the group. I wasn't done with my introduction when my phone rang. My shoulders slumped. I said, "Oh crap, it's probably my husband's doctor," and left the room.

I was mortified that I let such a word slip because I had a reputation for never swearing. And I was mad that I had this one opportunity to be in a caregivers' group and get some support, but a phone call snatched it from me. Caretaking was stressful, and it had gotten to me.

I didn't recognize it at first, but John's behavior started to change. My subconscious tried processing this in dreams at night. The first night, I dreamed that John and I were on an extensive road trip, and I was driving. At an intersection, I hesitated, and then proceeded. As soon as I drove on, I knew this was wrong. John had been passively sitting in the passenger seat, so I asked him to help by tracking our course on the map. This seemed to be a recognition that I wanted his guidance in these new circumstances.

The next night, I dreamed that John showed up with two rifles so we could go hunting. This was bizarre since we were both anti-gun and had never gone hunting in our lives. I think guns are scary. Did these guns represent my fear of what was happening to us?

The third night, I dreamed that John went to the grocery store. When he returned home with a persimmon, something we never ate, the store called wanting the SKU number off the sticker on the fruit. The sticker had fallen off, and John went frantically from room to room searching for it. Each time he didn't find it, he let out an explosive "F**k," which was very uncharacteristic of him. I questioned why they needed the information when he had already paid for it. And how did they get his phone number? I wonder if John's frantic hunt for the fruit label represented his desperate search for a cure or the reason he had gotten this illness. Persimmons were as foreign to us as bile duct cancer. After all, he hadn't done anything to deserve this in the dream or in real life. Why was he targeted by the store or the illness?

John was a very private person and didn't talk about his emotions or bodily functions. However, stressful situations can be a catalyst for behavior change. A couple of months before his death, I was sitting in our office doing some desk work. The room had two big windows that looked out on our front yard and walkway. John came in from the bedroom and said, "Look at this!" He dropped his pajama pants and said, "My scrotum and penis are huge!"

I was stunned, not because of the size of his genitals but because he was standing naked in front of the windows. This was so out of character. Clearly his illness had muted his inhibitions.

"Yeah, wow. I wonder what did that? We should call the doctor. Probably best to get away from the windows though," I said as I steered him back to the bedroom.

It took a phone call to the hospice nurse to find out that John's organs were breaking down and causing the fluid to build up in his belly.

John bravely took one day at a time. He lay in bed with his own thoughts, and I immersed myself in the tasks of caring for him. We were comfortable this way, living inside our own heads. It was easier not to express what we were feeling, even if we could articulate the swirl of thoughts in our brains. Talking about emotions was not a first language for either of us.

I never pressed him about his feelings, except once. After months, when I felt so alone and bereft not knowing his thoughts, I finally said, "I don't know how you are feeling. I've never done this. I want to take my cues from you, but I don't know what you are thinking. What are your thoughts about all this?"

"I think it's a pretty crappy situation," he said.

Those were the harshest words he said during his entire illness.

beginning of the end

After his second round of chemotherapy, John felt well enough to go to the theater to see an afternoon performance of Pilobolus, his favorite dance company. He did well but took a two-and-a-half-hour nap when we returned. His exhaustion also showed the next day when it took him an hour to get dressed, then it pulled him back into bed. He rose later to do a little work at his desk but slumped back to bed soon after.

Three weeks after John's second round of chemotherapy was done, we went to the hospital to meet John's new oncologist. His original oncologist had left recently for a job in Alabama, so his boss was taking over our case. Neither round of chemotherapy had halted John's cancer, so we were eager to talk about clinical trials. We were full of hope and willing to relocate anywhere to take advantage of a drug trial that might prolong John's life.

Grace was with us. She made monthly trips from Boston to Raleigh after John was diagnosed with his cancer. Today, we were in a large, sunny examining room. John sat while Grace and I stood or paced as we waited for the new doctor.

We took pictures of ourselves—Grace with her dad, me with John, John alone. In my favorite, I have bent over to put my cheek close to John's and my arms around his neck. He is very thin and, as we looked at the camera, he tried gamely to smile. These pictures make me weep today.

The new doctor was petite and young with a long ponytail. We were in our late sixties, so most of the staff seemed young. She spoke gently, but her words were surprising. "Mr. Watts, I have never met you before, but you look like a very sick man to me."

She noted that he looked very pale and probably needed a couple units of blood. She had his blood drawn on the spot. The results showed that she had guessed correctly. John was to return the next morning to get the blood infused. She also ordered a drain to be installed in his enlarged abdomen to reduce the excess fluid. Grace confided later that she thought her dad's enlarged belly made him look like he was pregnant.

The doctor told us that he was too sick for a clinical trial. Clinical trials for bile duct cancer were for people in the early stages of the disease. We were very disappointed, but the news got worse.

"I think it is time for you to enter hospice."

"Oh my god, I'm dying." John sobbed. It was as if she had punched him in the gut. Grace cried. I teared up to see John in pain. This was going in the opposite direction than what we had expected. He was only sixty-seven years old.

The doctor stood quietly as we pulled ourselves together. Then John said, "I know what I want to do. I want to die at home." So she placed an order for home hospice.

The doctor walked out of the room before we left. We readied ourselves to face the long walk out of the hospital into the outside world where our new reality waited. As we left, Grace saw the doctor in another room with her back to the doorway. She had been crying. It is a comforting thought to know that this doctor, who had been a stranger to us an hour before, could feel our loss, even though she had probably delivered bad news many times before. We rarely get to see our doctors this way. They seem so removed from our emotions because they are the rational voice in the room at times like these.

John, Grace, and I went out for Chinese food and ice cream when we left the hospital, but it was a somber meal. Since John had been off chemotherapy for a few weeks, he was feeling well enough to eat in a restaurant. But looking back, I wonder how we could have possibly eaten when we had received such terrible news. We must have been stronger than I remember. Or is it that we were on automatic pilot because shutting down was not a reasonable choice?

I don't know what we talked about at lunch; there wasn't much to say, but somehow we avoided long silences. As I drove us home, John stared out the window. The scenery whizzed by, and we passed a group of volunteers from our village picking up trash on the highway. John had been part of this crew months before.

"I wish I could still do that," he said.

His new reality seemed to come so suddenly. In the course of an hour, we had gone from optimism to staring at death. I didn't know much about hospice. Both my parents had had hospice services, but only for a week or less. Hospice meant we were on the last leg of the journey. I felt frozen with dread.

Four days after our fateful visit with the new oncologist, I had our close neighbors, Peg and Jim, over for brunch. John had told them early in his illness that he had cancer. Now he was telling them he was starting hospice. The meal went well, but as we sat around and chatted afterward in the living room, John dozed off in a lounge chair. Later in the afternoon, he rallied to sit at our dining room table and sort through family pictures. Even though Peg emailed after the visit that she thought John looked better than last time, by dinner time I noticed that he had faded, and his beautiful green eyes looked distant and dull.

The next weekend I went to the block party by myself. The chitchat went like this, "Where's John? We haven't seen him for a while."

"Oh, he's under the weather. He's had some back problems." I tried to be honest, but loyal to John's desire for privacy at the same time.

When I returned home, I told John, "People asked where you were. I told them you were having trouble with your back, but I'm not comfortable telling half-truths. I have to live with these people in the future. After you're gone, I don't want our neighbors to feel like I have been lying to them."

I was asking a lot of him. I was asking him to admit once more that he was dying. I was asking him to help make my future easier, a future he would never know. He graciously understood my feelings and conceded that it was time to tell the neighbors. Together we crafted the following email.

Dear Friends,

Many of you have asked me about John over the past few weeks. When he was diagnosed with a rare, aggressive bile duct cancer in late January, he decided to keep his illness private. Although doctors were able to alleviate his back pain, they were not able to eradicate the cancer. He has recently signed on to hospice care in our home. We expect to have family members coming and going over the next few weeks. We appreciated your concern, so I wanted to share this update with you.

Linda

Each reminder that I was losing John was like a mini-death, but I kept these feelings to myself. What was the point of expressing them? And to whom? John bore no responsibility here. I certainly didn't want to burden my friends or Grace. She was easily brought to tears when she thought of losing her dad. On one of her first visits, she broke down in the hospital waiting room while her dad was having radiation on his back.

"I always thought my dad would be alive to walk me down the aisle when I got married." She wiped the tears from her face. She was nowhere near getting married, but it was clear her fantasy of the future would need to change. She was adopted as a baby so had already lost one set of parents. Now she was losing her beloved father.

We were all losing. My hopes for the future needed to change too.

hospice

Once hospice began, our household was abuzz with activity. There was not much time to think. I just tried to keep us organized and react to John's needs. When he started to have balance issues, I bought him walking poles. His condition declined so quickly that the next day the hospice nurse ordered a walker. Within another few days he had a commode next to his bed. A couple of weeks more and he was in diapers. This situation reminded me of a recurring dream I had as a child where I was lying in the back seat of a driverless car that was whizzing down a hill. Only this time, hospice was in the driver's seat.

The hospice service had their own set of rules about what they did and did not provide. John would only receive palliative care, nothing to cure him. The hospice nurse was there to check on John, make sure he was comfortable, and advise us. I had to do all the daily nursing chores, but the nurse would show me what to do. In addition to her visits, a social worker and a chaplain came to the house. There were deliveries of medicine, equipment, and flowers. Family started arriving also.

At John's prompting, our son Henry arrived from California in mid-July for a few days. On this visit, John made sure they had a heart-to-heart talk before Henry left for the airport to go home. I'm sure they both knew it would be the last time they were together. Henry shared the following bits of conversation with me.

"We used to have a close relationship when you were little, but we seem to have drifted apart," John said.

Henry waited, then said, "What have you regretted most in life?"

"I wish I had had more friends, but you have been a good thing in my life."

"You certainly set me up well in life," Henry replied.

The day after Henry left, Dick and Jill Scobie, a couple from our Quaker meeting in Boston, arrived. We had been part of the meeting community for nearly thirty years, and members had sent cards and called while John was sick. I was very touched that they hadn't forgotten us since we had left Boston four years earlier. Certainly, we hadn't forgotten them. I was incredibly grateful to have the continued support of my Boston faith community. It only occurs to me now what a huge personal loss I experienced moving away from the meeting when we moved to North Carolina. At that time, I was looking forward to our new life. When I attended my last meeting for worship in Boston, I could not bear to enter the meeting room. I knew I would cry. I sat in the hall on a bench until a friend took my hand and led me in. It was so painful to think that I was leaving this community behind.

Dick and Jill were about fifteen years older than we were, and we had always looked to them for advice and wisdom. John declined most visits, but he enjoyed having this beloved couple in our home. Their gentle conversations were welcomed because they knew how to visit a dying man.

They stayed for four days and drove back to Boston with a box of books that John urged them to take. John was an avid reader, and his interests in sailboats and world history were different from mine. I wanted people to clean off the shelves for me, even though I was ambivalent as bits and pieces of John disappeared with his books.

In mid-July, John sat up in bed and watched Donald Trump's acceptance speech for the Republican nomination for president of the United States. A week later he watched Hillary Clinton's acceptance speech for the Democratic nomination, but he kept nodding off and asking me where we were in the speech. I was no help. I had no idea what the structure of her speech was.

"My biggest regret about dying is that I won't know how the election turns out." John said.

I thought to myself that if Trump won and John was still alive, I didn't want to be around. He avidly followed politics, and I know he would have been ranting after watching the news each night.

Our daughter Grace arrived the day before the Scobies left and stayed until her dad died. These ten days were a treasured time when John, Grace, and I could talk openly about his illness and impending death. During one such conversation, Grace was leaning against John's antique oak desk in our bedroom. I was sitting on the desk chair. Somehow the conversation turned to reincarnation. John was looking at Grace when he said, "I think I want to come back as a desk."

We laughed. What on earth was he thinking?

I hesitated, trying to follow his train of thought. "I suppose you could come back as a tree that gets made into a desk." No, he was adamant about coming back as a desk.

John was mostly lucid up to the end, but during the last two days, his breathing became labored and noisy. I slept on a mattress on our bedroom floor since the gel mattress for his bed sores took up most of our double bed. I wanted to be close, but his loud breathing was keeping me up at night. After a sleepless night, I moved my mattress into our walk-in closet. I was still within earshot, so this was not much improvement. Grace kept the guest room door open in case her dad called and I slept through it.

We didn't need a hospital bed for John because our adjustable bed allowed him to raise his head or feet at the touch of a switch. At night the buzz of the bed moving up and down as John tried to get comfortable roused me. I was so exhausted after nights punctuated with disturbances that I said, "John, you are deliberately moving your bed up and down just to wake me up every half hour!"

"I am not," he retorted. We had been reduced to bickering, a new low.

On his last two nights, John frequently called in a sing-songy voice, "Watermate? Where's my watermate?" When Grace or I appeared with a cup of water in hand, he cooed, "Ohh, there's my watermate!"

Grace and I found this absurdity very funny. I was operating on minimal sleep and trying to keep up with John's altered state of reality was making me punchy.

On Friday, the day before John died, his cousin Faye arrived from California. She had also visited in April and contributed to my efforts to clean up the yard by doing an extraordinary job of weeding the long, sloped bed of plantings. Faye shared our liberal values and had a quiet countenance that John and I appreciated. She was usually up before anyone else, drinking tea and reading on our screened porch.

Until her July visit, I didn't know that Faye had trained as a nursing assistant after high school. Her skills became incredibly helpful during John's last day and night. By the time she had arrived, his breathing was very labored. He was lucid, but not alert. He had developed bedsores and needed to be turned frequently. True to my straightforward style, I would just turn him without saying anything. Not Faye. She quietly said, "John, we are going to turn you to the left now. Are you ready?"

Wow, I thought. Of course, this is the respectful way to do this. Sometimes he groaned in pain, but I think we ultimately made him more comfortable. All day Saturday and into the evening, Faye, Grace, and I turned John and fluffed his pillows, feeling helpless to do much more. Faye tried reading to him, but he seemed to sleep through it.

John's raspy breathing continued into Saturday night, and he became restless and agitated. Our nurse had been there to check on him Tuesday, Thursday, and Friday. I called the after-hours hospice line. "John is acting uncomfortable and moving around a lot. Is there something I should give him?"

As instructed, I got a pill from the refrigerated box hospice had sent. I was told to place it under his tongue for fast absorption. John didn't seem conscious, so this concerned me. Back in the bedroom, I looked into his gaping mouth and said, "OK, John, I am going to place this pill under your tongue. Don't bite me."

I tucked the pill under his tongue and took my fingers away quickly. As I did, John snapped his teeth together three times in mock biting. Faye, Grace, and I chuckled in surprise. This was the last bit of humor John imparted.

He settled down, and we retreated to the kitchen. A few hours later, Faye slipped back down to the bedroom to check on John. She called to us. "Can you come here, please? John's breathing seems to have changed."

When my mother died, the hospital nurse called us at home to say, "Mrs. Patterson's condition has changed. You need to come to the hospital right away."

I said, "You mean she has died?"

"Her condition has changed," the nurse repeated.

As Grace and I walked down the hall to my bedroom, I reacted to Faye's comment about John's breathing. "That's the kind of thing they say when someone has died," I said. In retrospect, I hate admitting that I said this.

Faye stood next to the bed looking at John. "I can't tell if he is still breathing or not."

Grace and I stood and looked. "I think he is still breathing," I said. Then after a minute, "No, maybe he's not."

We went back and forth like this for about five minutes. Finally, I said, "Look, ladies, we need to make a decision." Faye checked his pulse. He was gone.

I stood at the foot of the bed, looking at my husband's lifeless body and said, "His mother did a fine job of raising him." Faye concurred. We stood there for a few minutes more, then discussed how to dress John for the trip to Duke University Medical School, where he was donating his body.

"Why put him in perfectly good clothes that will be discarded?" I said. "Let's just leave him in his diaper."

Silence. Grace and Faye didn't like that idea. One of them suggested dressing him in one of his prized long-sleeved Pogo shirts. This seemed appropriate. We moved his body gently as we pulled the shirt over his head and fed his arms into the sleeves. I remember thinking what a contrast dressing him in a Pogo shirt was to the way relatives used to wash and dress their loved ones in fancy outfits in the old days. I don't know what the protocol is for receiving bodies at Duke University, but I hope someone got a chuckle out of John's attire.

After we had John ready, I found tasks to keep myself busy. I put drops in his eyes so his corneas would not dry out before the eye bank could harvest them. I called the on-call hospice nurse to say that John had died, and I called the transport company to take him to Duke.

The nurse arrived and examined John's body. She also put drops in his eyes. She checked off the drugs we had left over and told us how to dispose of them. As she did her job, we stood there silently watching. I felt numb and drained. Grace suggested that I call Henry. I hesitated, "Oh, I don't know. Why don't you call him?"

Instinct told me that if I called him, I might lose what little composure I had left. I needed to be present, not to miss a second of what was going on with John. Grace said, "Mom, I really think you need to do this."

I called him. He was at a dinner party. When he saw that it was me, he stepped into the hall and took the call. We talked for five or ten minutes. He told me later that after our call, he sat quietly in the hall by himself before rejoining the party. He said something subtle, and a friend who knew what was going on gave him a hug. The party conversation continued.

A little while later, Grace received a text message from Henry's partner expressing his sympathy. I remember thinking how thoughtful that was.

As we watched the hospice nurse, the doorbell rang and two men dressed in suits arrived. They were respectful and expressed their condolences. Grace, Faye, and I stood in the bedroom and watched. The men suggested we leave the room while they transferred John's body to a stretcher. We declined. They explained that John would be kept in a refrigerated locker until he could be delivered to Duke University on Monday. I was concerned that he would be cold, even though I knew this thought was ridiculous.

I watched as they carried him through the house, down the front porch steps, along the brick walk, and into the darkness to their vehicle. I watched as they slid him in. I drank in every image to hold it close.

Back in the house, Grace and Faye murmured something about going to bed. It was around three in the morning. "Bed? No, I'm starved. Let's make waffles," I said. Grace dutifully went to the kitchen and whipped up a batch of whole-wheat waffles, my favorite kind.

We sat at the large oak dining room table that John had purchased a few months before he was diagnosed, a fitting locale for this meal. When I finally went to my room, I removed the gel mattress from the bed where John had lain earlier and changed the sheets. I climbed into bed and lay there letting the exhaustion sink in. I was delighted to be back in my own bed. I spread out my arms and legs feeling its emptiness and drifted off. My life as a widow had begun.

steeling myself

I have a low pain threshold. I have grabbed a drill out of a dentist's hand, signed up for all the technical bells and whistles before giving birth to my son, and have always been quick to see a doctor for any ache or pain. Avoiding pain, physical and emotional, is my nature. I avoid conflict and don't push boundaries. Sometimes I am slow to react and need time to digest a conflict or find the emotional space to deal with it. The entire six months that John and I dealt with his illness, I avoided facing my growing grief by maintaining a task-oriented approach to our lives. I didn't want to feel the emotion. I didn't want to feel the pain. I clung to my regular activities and our home routine to maintain my composure.

When John was confined to bed in his last month, I found it difficult to share my feelings. I avoided talking about how I would miss him or the good times we had enjoyed because I didn't want to cry in front of him. We could have cried together, but if I allowed myself to cry, I would have felt unhinged. It would have pushed open the door to my distress. I didn't want him to know that it hurt to know he was so sick. It hurt to know he would die soon. It hurt to think of my life without him. I didn't want him to feel guilt over leaving me. I wish I had been brave enough to share my feelings, but at the time I wasn't even able to identify them. I was scared and bracing myself. John must have felt a lot of emotional pain too. Unfortunately, we were never very good at sharing our deepest feelings. Maybe I walled him off by trying to maintain my composure. Maybe he was comfortable not talking about this devastating situation also.

Too late, I realized that even though John seemed unconscious in his last hours, he was still lucid. There was nothing inviting about his pose as he lay there with the air rushing noisily in and out of his mouth. During his illness he never encouraged me to pull up a chair and chat, so there seemed like no point then. As I have gotten further away from that night, I wish I had spent more time with him in this seemingly unreachable state. Now, I am able to imagine sitting next to his bed and rambling on about what a great life we had together. How much fun we had. What a terrific father he was. When I checked on him a few hours before he died, the one message I whispered in his ear was that if he needed to die, it was okay to let go. I didn't really want to lose him, but I had read that this was important. I was trying to do this right.

John died late Saturday night, July 30. I rose around six o'clock Sunday morning and emailed our Quaker meeting in Massachusetts announcing his death. Then I sent an email to our neighbors. After breakfast I started rearranging our walk-in closet to accommodate all the new equipment John had acquired from hospice—walker, commode, gel mattress, tray table. I also rearranged all of the clothes in the closet to make mine easier to access. Then I moved John's toiletries from his sink and replaced them with mine. I don't know why I thought his sink was better than mine. I wasted no time throwing out his old toothbrush, ointments, and combs. I washed out drawers and rearranged all the contents, keeping only what I thought I would use. I gathered his extra opioids to take to the police station and boxed up all the unused medical supplies for a friend's church to send overseas. All this activity gave me purpose, something to do, and a way to avoid my emotions. Although it seemed a little heartless at the time, in retrospect, I think I didn't want to wake up every morning and see his toothbrush, knowing that he would never use it again.

The only crack in my exterior came when Jerry, a neighbor, arrived Sunday morning with a large basket of food. He and his wife Elizabeth had gone out for breakfast before checking their email and didn't know that John had died the night before. They picked up groceries for us on the way home. He was surprised when I threw my arms around his neck and hugged him. Years later, when Jerry died of cancer, I refilled the same basket and took it back to Elizabeth.

Grace went back to Boston on Sunday afternoon, the day after John died. Cousin Faye stayed a few more days and was able to visit with John's sister, Peggy, who arrived on Monday. He had wanted to see his sister one more time, but she couldn't get a flight early enough.

John and Peggy's mother Phyllis had died a few months earlier in the spring, and her husband had shipped John boxes and boxes of family photos, mementos, and costume jewelry. John had gone through the jewelry with Grace and me and picked out a few pieces that he wanted me to have. Grace picked out pieces she liked, and he left the rest of the jewelry for his sister to distribute to her children and grandchildren. As cousins, Peggy and Faye spent hours at our dining room table sorting through family photos and dividing up the heirlooms.

I kept Peggy and Faye busy moving furniture when they weren't looking at photos. They helped me rearrange the heavy oak desks in the office John and I had shared. I preferred the placement of his desk, although many months later I realized that the original arrangement was better and moved the furniture back.

Peggy and Faye folded stacks of John's clothes for the local thrift store as I pulled his garments out of our closet. I put his shoes in bags and took his coats out of the hall closet. It was only when I started to take John's dress shirts off hangers that I suddenly stopped.

"That's it. I can't do any more. We're done," I said. Remembering John in the shirts he wore to work had a special meaning for me. These were the shirts I saw him in most. These were the shirts in which he looked the most handsome. The crisp white cotton with a delicate stripe or watch plaid set off his redhead complexion so nicely. I held on to those shirts for a year after his death and still have two of them today.

I will never know why I got rid of most of John's clothing so quickly after he died. This was in contrast to other people's styles of keeping their loved ones' wardrobes in the closet for years after their passing. I know of one woman who never made the bed that her husband died in for years after his death. Nor did she sleep in the room, much less clean out his closet. A good friend kept his wife's effects in the secret hope that she would return. I held a different fantasy. I got rid of John's things because I wanted to forget the pain of losing him.

After Faye went home, Peggy and I were the only ones left. She seemed ready to take care of me, but I didn't feel like I needed any care. I was quite self-sufficient except for needing help moving heavy furniture. Still, I appreciated her presence because it eased the transition from having had a busy household for the last month to the deadly silence of being alone.

My father died two years after my mother died. He had a stroke on the anniversary of her death and another one a couple of weeks later on her birthday. He lived another eight months in that condition before he passed away. There are countless stories of spouses dying within days, weeks, and months of each other. I was terrified of this fate. I steeled myself against an early demise. I was determined to be a survivor.

I didn't want to become depressed, unable to get out of bed. I feared slipping into a dark pit. Having had brief visits by the dark ghost at other transitions in my life—leaving college, being fired from a job—I was determined to power through to the other side of grief. I maintained an upbeat attitude and often heard myself laughing. One friend referred to me as Pollyanna.

I wasn't surprised that I took charge during John's illness or after his death. When I am confronted with a threat or a challenge, my systems go into overdrive, and I am on high alert. Only when I feel safe, do I let down my guard and perform at my usual level. I maintained my self-assurance for months by keeping busy. Activity distracted me from my loss. I was not afraid to do things by myself and enjoyed my new freedom and perspective. I was determined not to let John's death bring me down.

two memorial services

The month John was in hospice care, I started planning his memorial services. I intended to have one in Boston at our Quaker meeting and another in North Carolina for our local friends. I pondered different local venues. We were not associated with a Quaker meeting in North Carolina, so holding his service in a nearby meeting house didn't seem right. Neither did the event space in our village restaurant. I remembered a roped-off stairway with a sign that said "Community Room" in the local bookstore. I went to look at it, but the large leather chairs placed around the long table looked more appropriate for a corporate board meeting. I asked about the back room of the bookstore where speakers presented their books to small audiences. With its walls lined with bookshelves, it seemed like a perfect place for John's memorial service. This room was available. I was delighted.

Several years earlier, I supported the local library's fundraiser by purchasing an engraved patio block for John's birthday that said "John C. Watts, Lover of Cats and Books." I love walking by that block every time I enter the library. At the time of purchase, I had no idea of the meaning it would hold in my future.

I told John what I was planning for his services. He was surprised I was planning two, and even more surprised that I was holding one in our village bookstore. He said, "Who would come?" He would have been surprised that the local memorial service was standing room only. Friends and neighbors filled the fifty chairs we set out, and his workmates lined the back of the room.

I wanted to create a pamphlet for John's memorial services. This was easy for me since I spent the bulk of my career as a graphic designer. I picked out a favorite picture and talked to him about what should be included in his biography. He seemed pleased to be involved. I sat next to his bed as he recounted what seemed like every detail from his high school years to the present. I dutifully took notes, knowing that I would need to heavily edit his life story to fit the page.

Grace suggested making a photo book for guests to view at John's memorial services. I picked out my favorite photos, arranged them on the pages, and ordered four photo books at my local CVS. Unfortunately, they ran out of covers. There seemed to be no covers in North Carolina, so I ended up ordering them in Boston. Grace transported the photo books when she came to North Carolina for John's first service.

John wanted to have the poem "the lesson of the moth" by Don Marquis read at his services. I had never heard it before I met him, but it must have held special meaning for him since he was dying at a relatively young age. The poem talks about a moth that chooses to immolate himself to experience the beauty of fire instead of leading a long, unexciting life. I have never understood his attachment to this poem because he led a relatively stable life, other than his cross-country bike trip in his twenties. Maybe he yearned for more excitement in his life.

John had also requested that I play three songs at his service: "Cavatina" from the movie *The Deer Hunter*, John Lennon's "Imagine," and the Henry Mancini Orchestra and Chorus's version of "Somewhere Over the Rainbow." I listened to each of these, although I was very familiar with the first two. John had loved Henry Mancini since his teenage years and had a complete collection of his work. Unfortunately, the Mancini version of Judy Garland's hit was so dated and insipid I couldn't bear it. What's more, it did not mesh with the mellowness of the instrumental "Cavatina" and Lennon's gentle "Imagine." I only played the two songs. If he haunted me for this omission, so be it.

Putting together the services and creating the pamphlet and photo books were a comfort to me. Having meaningful projects that used my professional skills grounded me and gave me purpose. I may not have known what my future held, but at the time, I felt secure because I knew how to write and design a brochure, lay out pictures, and plan an event.

Both services were to be held in the manner of the Society of Friends. One of the things I treasure about Quaker memorial services is the participation of the attendees. After a period of silence, guests are free to stand up and share a remembrance or a story about the deceased. I gained insight into how John's workmates saw him through their stories in the cozy North Carolina bookstore service. One co-worker described how much John had helped her with a project. Another mentioned that John's nickname at work was MegaWatts. Some of their stories were laced with work humor. Grace was so touched by what they said, she wished her friends who attended the service in Boston could have heard these tributes. I will always be grateful for his co-workers' presence and remembrances, revealing a side of my husband I could not have known.

We had the same opportunity in Boston. Here, many of John's Boston workmates cast him as the life of the party during their lively political lunch discussions, times John thoroughly enjoyed. I had placed John's obituary in the newspaper from Needham where we had lived for twenty-four years, but I was surprised to see so many old friends and neighbors. I was particularly touched by our friend Susan who attended from New Jersey. She took the train to Boston and back in one day. When she was a college student at MIT, she had been Korean-born Grace's "Korean big sister."

Henry flew into Boston from Bulgaria, where he was working at the time. At one point during the service, he took my hand and squeezed it. Grace sat to his right. We must have filed into the meeting room in that order because I would have preferred to have my children on either side of me. I was pleased that Henry rose to speak. This is what he said:

When someone dies, your relationship with them immediately changes—you're not trying to fit them into your life anymore. You're suddenly opened up, trying to take everything that was good about them and let it live through you. To make sure the world still gets the benefit of their strengths, some way, somehow.

There are a lot of things my father wasn't. He wasn't effusive. The room didn't light up when he walked in. We were not emotionally close—there weren't any emergency phone calls for fatherly advice or fishing trips to the mountains. During his illness, he told me that his biggest regret was that he didn't have many close friends, a worry I also share in my own life. And despite his calm, peacemaking personality, the things that stressed him out could take him from zero to furious in very little time—also something I struggle with.

But even as I see in his example some things I hope will go differently in my life, so many of the things that I'm most proud of in myself, I got from him. The last thing my father ever said to me was 'you've been such a good thing in my life,' and I want everyone who knew and cared about him to know the ways he was a good thing in mine.

My father was a doer and a teacher. He was good with both his mind and his hands. My lifelong relationship with computers started with him patiently letting me take apart and reconfigure our home computer, confident that he could fix anything I really messed up. We never called plumbers or electricians—he would take broken

41

pieces down to our basement and fix them. When I left for boarding school, he gave me a small bag of tools—just in case—something I'd need someday. I didn't use them very often, but years later, when my car wouldn't start at a gas station thousands of miles from home, I used the wire strippers from that first bag (either foolishly or bravely) to rewire the ignition system. We were moving again within the hour. The wire strippers came in handy, for sure, but the conviction that I could do it myself came directly from my father.

My father was silly. He wasn't talkative or outgoing, but he was theatrical in his own way. He'd make jokes, do impressions, and graft personality and voices onto stuffed animals (and our cats). He performed in musicals.

My father was up for anything. I've loved cars my whole life, and he took me to the auto show every year. Even after I'd gone to college, he went by himself one year because he knew I'd appreciate having all the sales brochures. He'd rarely say no to what my sister and I wanted to do. One thing I especially remember from my childhood was our nightly 'activity.' Almost every night for years, my parents would spend an hour or so with us before our bedtime, doing whatever we wanted. Playing with cars, drawing, doing all sorts of things that I imagine now must have been boring for adults. I don't know to what extent most parents make this amount of time to play with their children, but looking back, I can only be surprised and grateful at the consistency with which it happened.

He was smart, supportive, and could do things a lot of people can only dream of doing, and he spent thirty years giving me those things in any way he could. We all stand on the shoulders of those who have come before us—his were some great shoulders.

I had been frustrated by Henry's reserve during John's illness, but hearing his words washed all my disappointment away. I needed to be reminded that he didn't talk any more easily about his feelings than his father did. And, like John, he wasn't effusive. I was glad to hear all that he appreciated about his dad.

My planning paid off. I was able to attend each memorial service without worrying about last minute details. I was able to offer John all the respect he was due and to relax and absorb all the tributes paid to him. I found the composure to speak at both services. And I soaked up all the support I was offered.

navigating without a map

How does a person without traditional religious faith find their way through grief? So many people turn to religion in times of life's traumas. I imagine for believers, there is reassurance in knowing that there is a plan or that a spiritual power is taking care of them and their loved ones. Much of the consolation and advice offered after someone's passing is couched in religious terms or a belief in an afterlife. "He's with God now." "Don't worry because you will see him again when you die." I had a neighbor who told her husband not to fear death because in Heaven he would be healed and could play golf as much as he wanted.

None of this has ever made sense to me. What if you were married twice? Is your second spouse's first partner going to be happy to see you in Heaven? My brother was married five times. How does that work? Some people welcome the map of religious thought to guide them through the fog of bereavement, but I didn't.

My early life was full of missteps in regard to religion. I grew up in the Presbyterian church and got off on the wrong foot with my Sunday school teacher when, as a preschooler,

I used an inappropriate word to describe Jesus. Later, during a service, the music box in my new yellow plaid purse played "How Much is That Doggie in the Window?" when I unsnapped it to take out my offering. As a seven-year-old, I enjoyed singing in the junior choir but didn't always understand what the words meant. Every Easter we sang the "Battle Hymn of the Republic."

Mine eyes have seen the glory
Of the coming of the Lord;
He is trampling out the vintage
Where the grapes of wrath are stored;
He hath loosed the fateful lightning
Of His terrible swift sword;
His Truth is marching on.

Grapes of wrath? Terrible swift sword? His truth is marching? What did this mean? I'm still not sure, but I now know that the "Battle Hymn of the Republic" was written by Julia Ward Howe as a pro-Union, anti-slavery anthem during the Civil War. No wonder I was confused.

When I was a teenager, I was asked to play the piano as the senior high Sunday school sang hymns. I knew I would tense up and not do well. I tried to get out of it to no avail. Despite practicing the songs, I spent two agonizing weeks of hesitating and struggling through chords. I was not asked to play again. What a relief.

Very occasionally, the minister, a tall, balding man with wire-rimmed glasses and a quiet demeanor, graced the senior high Sunday school class with his presence. I gathered my courage to ask him a question that had bothered me for years. Before he vanished into his office downstairs, I stopped him and said, "Why does God let so many people suffer?" He said that God was too far away in Heaven to help us down here on earth. My faith suffered a huge blow that day.

Despite my failure to accept my Presbyterian upbringing, I was still curious about religion. In college I sent away for weekly devotional pamphlets from Norman Vincent Peale, a pastor in New York City and the author of *The Power of Positive Thinking*.

Sometime in my twenties, on a lark, I attended a Quaker meeting in Brooklyn, New York. I remember sitting in the silence of that meeting for worship and feeling like this experience was the start of something new for me. I liked the quiet. No one was lecturing me, no one required me to repeat prayers or responsive readings that meant nothing to me. There was no pastor and no dogma, just values of integrity, equality, simplicity, community, stewardship, and peace. No creeds, only queries or questions to guide personal and group reflection. And no set definition of god or spirit. The Quaker identity as seekers resonated with me.

Individual Quakers hold a broad spectrum of thoughts about God from belief in the Trinity to more universalist leanings and everything in between. I believe there may be value in all religions. I prefer to think of myself as an agnostic, because I don't know if there is a god or not. I think it is presumptuous for anyone to think they can define God. However, this does not keep me from being curious about a spiritual life.

I wanted to be at the hospital with my mother when she passed away. An African hospice worker once told me that you can see the spirit leave the body, and I wanted to see if this was true.

My father and I spent the night on cots next to my mother's bed as she labored to breathe. At six a.m., my father said, "Linda, take me home. I didn't get any sleep."

"What!" I said. "Mother is so close to death."

"I don't care," he said. "I am tired."

Reluctantly, I drove him home where we both slept until the hospital called around ten a.m. to say we needed to come back. My mother had died, and I had missed it.

When we arrived at the hospital, I was able to spend a little time with my mother's body. I told the hospice worker that I liked the way she had combed my mother's hair and asked, "Did you see my mother's spirit leave her body?"

"No." she said.

"Have you ever seen anyone's spirit leave their body?"

"No, never" was the answer.

When my father and I retreated to the hospital cafeteria, we sat awkwardly and sipped coffee as my dad said over and over, "I can't believe it." I did not offer my father any empty platitudes. What was there to say? This was my first direct experience with death. All I could offer was my care and companionship. Later that day, my father modeled what I would later imitate as a way to respond to grief. He dressed in a suit and tie and went to the church to have his picture taken for the church directory. He had scheduled his appointment weeks ago and didn't want to miss it. I was mystified by his

47

behavior at the time, just as I was mystified by my own behavior after John died.

A couple of evenings later, my father sat in his home office as I sat on the stool at my mother's desk in the kitchen. The closed door to the basement lay in the short hall between us. Suddenly my father called to me sharply, "Linda, do you have a door open? There is a draft in here."

There were no doors open. The basement was heated so there would not be a draft. He continued to complain until I rose and walked toward his office. As I walked into the hall, I felt the cold air. It was unmistakable. I walked closer to my father, and it was gone. To this day I believe it was my mother's spirit.

As a Quaker, I have learned to trust the small, quiet voice within me. When my mother died, I was moved to design a brochure with pictures of her on the inside and my pet names for her on the cover. I wanted to make these pamphlets available at her memorial service. My brother didn't like this idea, but I needed to produce this piece of art to express my feelings of loss.

Two years later, I lost my father. He had been a member of the church choir for more than thirty years. At his memorial service, I asked the choir director to end the service with one of my favorite pieces, their rendition of Lutkin's "The Lord Bless You and Keep You."

When they sang the musical benediction, I closed my eyes as tears streamed down my face. I let the sublime music and memories of my father reverberate through my body. We had been close, and the pain of loss was sharp and deep.

Part way through the song, I felt a hand under my elbow. It was the pastor. He had started to recess and wanted to escort me down the aisle. I stood my ground. This was my moment to savor the music and grieve my loss. The pastor was insistent, and not wanting to make a scene, I gave in and followed his lead out of the pew. He hustled my family down the aisle and into the church garden where my father's ashes were interred.

In retrospect I smolder with disappointment. I was robbed of the last minutes of the song, the beautiful intertwining amens that gave me chills. This was the last time I would ever stand in that church grieving my father, holding him close as I listened to this blessing. This was a spiritual, transcendent moment for me that was interrupted by religious protocol.

Months after my father died, he stood at the foot of my bed and looked at me. He seemed more real than a dream. I had the sense he was checking to make sure I was okay or telling me he was okay. Then, he was gone. He never came back in that form.

While John was in hospice, he said, "I wish I believed in God and an afterlife, but I just don't. I admire people who have those beliefs. It must be a comfort to them." He received an email from a co-worker who wanted to talk to him and bring him to Jesus before he died. John wrote back telling the man what his beliefs were and added, "Sorry, but I don't need to talk to you. After sixty-seven years, I have had many people try to convert me. Obviously, their efforts have not worked."

John was rarely this blunt, but proselytizing was not what he needed on his death bed.

After John died, I had no religious faith to comfort me. No hope that I would see him in the afterlife. This didn't bother me because we had been in harmony about our beliefs. I had the confidence that I was resilient and creative and would find a way forward. Although I did not believe in a master plan, I held on to the idea that life for me was not over. I had a future, and I needed to be strong to meet it. Ayn Rand had said, "All growth demands destruction." All things change, and it was up to me to listen to the small voice within and realign my universe.

My experiences with what I believed were my parents' spirits are as close as I have gotten to belief in an afterlife. Some people say that their deceased loved one watches over them from Heaven. I have never believed in angels. However, I played with the idea in the second year after John's death. I was feeling very upset after spending a week on a cruise populated with couples. I felt so alone. The first day back, emotional fatigue kept me from going to the gym and choral practice. I felt like crying constantly. The only appointment I kept was with a doctor to treat my urinary tract infection.

I felt so exhausted and weepy I skipped my bereavement group the next night. I never missed my bereavement group; it was a lifeline for me. About nine that night, I received a call saying that one of the people I usually carpooled with had fallen down a flight of stairs and ended up in the emergency room. Members of the bereavement group went to the hospital with her, but eventually slipped away home as the evening wore on. She checked herself out of the hospital at one a.m.

If I had attended that evening, I would have been sitting in the emergency room all evening, miserable and exhausted.

The next day I still felt weepy and fatigued and spent most of the day in bed. I forced myself to get up and drive to my voice lesson. I was met at the door by my voice teacher in her bathrobe. She had the flu. As I returned to my car, I whispered, "Thank you, John." He had been my angel.

Before the deaths of my parents and husband, I thought that when a person died, they ceased to exist. Now I see that loved ones leave traces of their lives in unexpected ways. I have integrated family memories into my thoughts, but my home is also graced with objects from their lives. A grandfather clock that my dad made from a kit stands in my house. Another one of his clocks sits on my fireplace mantel. A crock that my mother, as a child, decorated with wrapping paper bits and shellacked is displayed on one of the built-in shelves in my living room. Her prized antique spool cabinet, taken from an old store, sits in my living room also.

I have a collection of my grandfather's handicrafts that I treasure. He taught shop skills in a prison. He fashioned doll bureaus for his daughters from tin and painted them brown. They have mirrors, doors that open, and drawers that pull out. My favorite item is the miniature log cabin he made with double hung windows with glass panes that slide up and down, each piece made from metal that he painted to look like wood. The front door opens to reveal a sliding trough for incense so smoke comes out of the chimney. I have a mission oak child's rocker that he crafted and a primitive inlaid side table with carved scallops along the top edge that one of his prison students made. I don't know how my grandfather came to possess this marvelous table, nor do I know anything about this prisoner. I keep it as a reminder that, in or out of prison, there is some good in all of us, a Quaker concept.

My house is filled with memories of my husband too: antique furniture we bought together; jewelry he had given me; hand-thrown pottery received as wedding gifts displayed on shelves; and tucked in my bureau, the short-shorts he liked me to wear that no longer fit. All of these items make me feel connected to something bigger than myself. They and my memories help define a place for me in a larger family.

Besides the behaviors and talents my parents fostered in me, the most surprising legacy has been food cravings. My mother, a home economics teacher, was always enthusiastic about food. One of her favorites was Caesar salad. It never appealed to me until years after her death. Then it became the only salad I ordered. She was always eating nuts, and now I eat nuts every day. And recently, I have had a craving for pickled beets, a favorite dish from my mother's Pennsylvania German upbringing.

My grief for John has been very different from my grief for my parents. I am reminded every day that John is gone. As a young adult, I grew away from my parents and built a life with John. When my parents died, I was somewhat protected from the loss because of the distance in our daily lives. They were in their eighties, so it seemed like the natural cycle of life to eventually lose them.

There are so many layers when we lose someone who is a part of our daily lives. Superficially I had to find new ways to do things. Television became my new dinner companion. If I needed something fixed, I learned to do it myself or to call a handyman. Only after I proved to myself that I could survive on my own did I allow myself to feel the loss of my spiritual union with John. It was six months before he came to me in a dream. I don't remember the details, just that he was smiling, and I was glad to see him.

hospice bereavement group

The hospice chaplain signed me up for her eight-week group soon after John died at the end of July, but it didn't start until the end of October. Three months seemed like a long time to wait. I was more than ready, hoping to be cured or at least healed. I expected some prescribed way to grieve to relieve me of my disquiet.

The session started out like most groups—we introduced ourselves and said a few words about our situations. Three of us were widows and one, a widower. Our two group leaders brought worksheets and led discussions each week. We always ended each hour-and-a-half session with a poem that was like dessert after a meal.

I was very enthusiastic about this support opportunity, but I don't think I was ready to accept all of the concepts presented. I am reminded of the adage, "You can bring a horse to water, but you can't make it drink." For example, we were told that it was a common myth a bereaved person should "get over it" and distract themselves with activities. It may have been a myth, but it was my automatic reaction to getting through my grief. Just hearing that it was a myth was not enough to sway me from my natural course. It seemed like it was working for me. Another idea suggested that our loved one would always be part of us. This surprised me. If John was always with me, how could I move on? I was trying to block out the pain of loss, not bring it along. It took me years before I saw the truth in this.

I was surprised that we had to fill out worksheets for this group. I wasn't expecting to have to think or do any work, much less homework. The activities forced me to delve into my feelings and memories, and ponder what I had lost—all the collateral losses and the roles John and I had filled for each other. I made lists of our strengths, coping mechanisms, and my needs. I learned about self-care. One of the most difficult tasks was completing thoughts like:

When you died, I felt…

I feel sad for the future because…

One thing I want you to know is…

The first phrase left me speechless. I had no idea how I felt. I was not in tune with that side of myself. I wanted to answer the second by writing, "I feel like screaming." I drew a blank on the third phrase, one thing I want you to know. This was a good exercise because it made me aware of how out of touch I was with my feelings.

One of my favorite activities was writing metaphors and similes about my experience of grief. I wrote: grief is like an autumn day when the leaves start to fall. And, grief is like the undertow at the seashore. I enjoyed this so much I wrote a poem and shared it with the group.

I donated your clothes
And took over your closet,
Rearranged your folders
in our shared file cabinet.

I cleaned out your wallet
And put it in a drawer,
Closed your checking accounts
And cut up your credit cards.

I sold your blue Toyota
And cleaned out the garage.
I go to the theater alone
And sit next to a stranger.

I use the sink that was yours.
And sprawl across our bed at night.
I don't watch your favorite shows,
But claim your iPhone as mine.

As our life together dissipates
And I am carried forward by the days,
Sweet memories of you appear
Like reflections on the windows of a train.

Another exercise was to list everything of significance I had ever lost—old loves, jobs I outgrew, jobs I never got, relationships with friends and relatives that faded from neglect. We were told that one major loss brought up other losses, collateral losses. Mourning could compound. I made my list, but the full impact of this concept didn't hit me until the end of our sessions.

One of those old losses came back into my life about a week before John died. I had a full house with the Scobies and Grace. As I cooked dinner, my flip phone buzzed fourteen times as I received fragments of a long text from an old college boyfriend I hadn't seen in about forty years.

These interruptions were particularly annoying because, before John, this guy had been the love of my life. Why was he texting me? The only contact I had had with him since college was when I emailed his wife a couple of years ago to express sympathy over a tragedy that befell them. At the time, he responded by thanking me for reaching out. That was it. So why contact me now?

Despite my exhaustion, I pieced together the fragments of his texts and emailed him a reply after dinner.

Dear Phil,

You sent me fourteen jumbled text messages tonight— could be my non-smart phone. Please don't text me. I don't text. I don't have much sense of humor these days either, since my husband is in hospice. Sounds like you have troubles too. I'm sorry to hear that your marriage is ending in divorce.

Too tired to say much more,
Linda

He sent back a more civilized response than mine and asked if he could call me. He called a night or two later. We had an awkward conversation about the old days in college. I asked why he had called me. He said that he had always felt especially close to me. Did I remember that night we talked for hours on the roof of the art hall? I honestly didn't. He told me he was separated from his wife and that he had a girlfriend of six months. In fact, he said, he had dated over twenty women in the past year since his marriage broke up.

"Wow, where do you meet that many women?" I said.

"They're my patients," he said. He used to be a primary care doctor but had gone into the aesthetic side of medicine, giving Botox shots and laser treatments. In fact, he had undergone these treatments himself. He wanted to Skype. I said no. Knowing what he did for a living made me suddenly self-conscious about the scars on my face that I acquired in childhood. I was in no mood to worry about my appearance. He asked if he could call me again. I remembered Phil as a very empathetic guy and had no reason to say no. He continued to call me every so often for months. Even though his calling me seemed strange since he had a girlfriend, he was a wonderful source of comfort in the early months of my widowhood. I appreciated the attention, and he made me feel valued.

During our conversations, we talked about old times, cleared up old wounds (his parents didn't hate just me, they hated any woman he got close to) and talked about our children, John, and Phil's two previous wives. After months, he started telling me how he remembered what great legs I had and asked if I remembered making love under the boardwalk at the beach. No, I hadn't remembered that either.

Eventually my old feelings for Phil started to surface to the point where they obscured the fact that he had a girlfriend. One night in November I perused his Facebook site and was jolted back to reality. There under status, it said "in a relationship" and the name of the woman he had told me about. I felt flattened.

This was one of those "other" losses that the current loss might bring up again. I was so confused I couldn't hold it together during our next hospice bereavement group session. I sobbed and choked. Who was I crying for—John or Phil—my husband or the loss of an old love? Or was I crying from the stress of confusion? Phil's attentions had hijacked my grief process. I had hoped to skip over the sad work of grief by going straight into a new relationship. Although Phil seemed supportive, I began to wonder what his motivations were. Even so, we continued our occasional calls.

The hospice group ended in November with a session on surviving the holidays. I was not worried. I had a plan. I was going to Washington, DC, by myself for Thanksgiving and meeting my daughter, son, and his boyfriend in San Diego at Christmastime. My concern was for the future. I was like a colt on wobbly legs. The hospice group was over, but I still needed support. I felt the need to meet regularly with people who had the same concerns I did. After the group ended, three of us from the hospice bereavement group got together once in my living room. Another member and I saw each other in the health club regularly, but other than that, I was alone to sort out my feelings. Alone and not even close to being healed.

adult children

People respond differently to the loss or grave illness of a parent. Our reactions can be colored by our relations with them over the years: good times, strong bonds, slights, misunderstandings, personality clashes, and our maturity level. My mother died when I was forty-eight. We never got along very well, but when she was scheduled for colon cancer surgery, I called her every night. I wanted to emotionally support her, to let her know that I cared despite our differences, and perhaps to hold on to some last moments with her in case the surgery didn't go well.

When I was in my twenties, she had had a brain tumor. My dad called me to say that she would have surgery in early December and that she had a fifty percent chance of survival. I was stunned and not sure what to say. I had started a new job 350 miles away and could not take off work to be with her when she returned from the hospital. At that point in my life, I don't think it occurred to me to call her; I relied on my father's reports.

When I visited at Christmas, I surprised and delighted my mother by bringing Christmas cookies I had made in my tiny

Boston apartment since my mother was not able to bake that year. When I went to her bedroom, she was sitting up in bed. She had a certain style about her that skirted the more tender issues in life. She whipped off her wig and said, "You want to see my scar?" There on her bald head was a large horse-shoe-shaped scar. Quite a greeting, but that was my mother.

She recovered well, but my guilt of not going home for her surgery dogged me for years. Ten years later I tried to tell her how sorry I was and to give her a hug, but she pushed me away.

My children responded to John's illness in very different ways. Grace is a heart-centered person. She was always emo-tionally available and gave me a lot of support by checking in regularly. She even taught me to text so we could stay in touch more frequently. Henry is head-centered and more re-served. His reactions were more difficult to discern.

Grace's devotion during her father's illness mirrored my devotion to my father in his last days. After my dad had a series of strokes, I flew from Boston to Philadelphia every month; in the months leading to his death, I was there nearly every week. After John's diagnosis in January, Grace flew from Boston to North Carolina almost monthly when she was able to get time off from her job as a social worker. Sometimes she was able to attend a medical appointment with us and some-times we just spent time together at home. Her presence was hugely comforting. It was nice to be able to casually chat or to get her help with chores. She climbed ladders and took boxes off shelves that I couldn't reach, and she helped me in the yard to terrace a small garden and to pick up pinecones and sticks. John and I were delighted to have her with us.

There were activities that John and I had always wanted to do but hadn't gotten around to: visiting the Outer Banks, going kayaking or canoeing, and taking Grace to an expensive restaurant we enjoyed in our village. Every time she visited during those months, I mentioned one of these activities, but John was never enthusiastic.

On one of her visits, we drove out in the country to a canoe launch, but as we neared, I realized how unrealistic a canoe ride would be. Even if John could get into the canoe (and he couldn't), he was too sick to enjoy it. If the unthinkable happened and we tipped over, Grace and I wouldn't have been able to save him, a horrible thought. I vetoed the canoe ride. Grace was angry. I didn't blame her. I always had high hopes that we would do something fun, but John was too ill for fun.

A year or so after John died, Grace, her boyfriend, and I spent a week in a beachfront condo on the Outer Banks. And the summer after that, following a memorial service at Duke University for anatomical gift donors, I took her to the upscale restaurant that John and I enjoyed. We still haven't gone canoeing.

John was very open about his illness with his children and extended family. Grace recalls him calling her before his tests were conclusive and saying that it looked bad: he might have cancer. Henry, who lived in California, remembers driving with his boyfriend when John called to report he had a diagnosis, bile duct cancer. Years after John died, I asked Henry what he felt at the time, but didn't get an answer. Could I remember what I had felt when my dad called me to say that my mother had a brain tumor or that my grandmother had died? I don't think I was sympathetic enough when my grandmother died when I was a college student, but I do remember feeling the gravity of possibly losing my own mother. When my father called me before my mother's surgery, he was upset, so his emotion was contagious.

At twenty, we don't have the same perspective that we have later in life when we may have experienced more losses. Henry was thirty when John died, but when he was in his twenties, he lost a friend. Long after their romance was over, one of the loves of his life committed suicide. Henry visited his friend's Facebook site from time to time, and on one of those occasions, he saw condolence messages. Henry honored his friend at the Burning Man Festival in Nevada by placing his friend's picture in the temple that goes up in flames each year.

Henry is an introvert and has never shared his feelings easily, but he is an articulate person who can argue me into a corner. He has always been dutiful and called on birthdays and holidays, but he has never shared his emotional side with us except when his pent-up frustration or anger boiled over every few years. I know he feels things deeply. I know this from the long, strong hugs he gives me when we part after our Christmas visits. I know this from the sweet note he wrote me in a Christmas card the December after John died. And I know because he took my hand at a poignant moment during John's memorial service.

However, I didn't know what he was feeling during the six months of John's illness. He was caught up in job interviews in the early months. When I emailed, he kept me apprised of the companies he had interviewed with and the outcomes, but I don't remember receiving any emails or calls saying, "How's Daddy?" In February, Grace was visiting for John's birthday. I felt fiercely protective of John and couldn't understand why Henry hadn't called by the evening. Forgetting about the three-hour time difference between North Carolina and California, I went into another room and sent him this email:

All of Daddy's far-flung relatives have called, emailed, sent cards, and expressed their concern directly to him. There has been one relative absent. You asked what you could do to help—emotional support is something you can offer. And today is his birthday. You have always been so good about calling on holidays. You might not have too many more chances.

– Mom

His email reply:

I was about to call him, but thanks for the guilt-ridden, dramatic email anyway.

Still, I was baffled by Henry's seeming lack of emotion and interest in his dad's welfare. It may be that he modeled what he learned from his parents and grandparents. I came from a family of people who preferred not to deal with emotional situations. I had learned the craft well. John's family was warm but lived out west and we had little contact with them. John grew up without a father in the household and was usually reluctant to share his sensitive side.

Henry may not have spoken with me or Grace about his father's illness and impending death, but in time, it was clear he was affected. A year and a half after John's death, I purchased a beautiful vessel for John's ashes. I was so excited and wanted to share it with someone, but who would want to come over and see an urn I had just purchased for my late husband? I took a picture of it and texted it to Henry and Grace. They both responded quickly with positive comments. Henry added, "Speaking of handmade things with a personal meaning, here's a picture of a cutting board I made." The tiny picture showed a beautiful cutting board made from layers of different woods. I was gobsmacked.

As a child, Henry had shown little interest in woodworking beyond scout projects and middle school shop class. Grace could be found in our basement, hammer in hand, making a pinball machine with rubber bands and nails, but Henry would be in his room deep into the world of software. When he sent the picture, I replied, "Henry that is fantastic! What possessed you to make this?"

"I took a furniture making class and this was the first project," he texted.

"I am so excited. Your dad was a woodworker, my father was a woodworker. This is so terrific."

This may seem like an extreme reaction, but my feelings about woodshops run deep. When I was a small girl, I wanted to be with my dad even when he was working with his power tools in the basement. The scream of the table saw terrified me, so I put my hands over my ears and hid in a large wooden box my dad had made to cover the saw when not in use. I became very familiar with my father's workbench and all the tools hanging on the inside of the cupboard he built. I can still smell the sawdust of fresh cut wood in his shop.

Like a lot of parents, I check Facebook to see what my children are up to. Henry had posted a picture of his cutting board creation. This picture was clearer than the one he had texted me earlier. There was something eerily familiar about it. I realized that there was a tiny knot near one of the corners. His father had also made a cutting board from layers of wood when he was in high school. He had gotten an A- on it because there was a knot near one of the corners of his board. I still had this chopping block so I know Henry had seen it. Wow, I thought. He does remember his father.

About six months after Henry made the cutting board, I received a text in the middle of the night. It had a picture of a moose and said, "We've only been in Alaska seven hours and already we have seen a moose!"

I propped myself up on one elbow and thought, I didn't even know you were going to Alaska. I roused myself and texted back, "You must be channeling your father. He always wanted to see a moose."

He responded, "I know. That's why I sent the picture."

He had remembered our family trip to Maine when John was so determined to see a moose. We loaded in the car at dusk and drove into the woods until long after dark. Creeping along, we realized that we were on an extremely narrow bridge with no side rails. We were crossing a large lake, barely visible in the dark, and the water lapped at our tires. If we stepped out of the car or drove slightly off course, we would be in the lake. We had no idea where we were going. I was extremely nervous. Eventually we came to a main road and made it back to our hotel. John never saw a wild moose on that trip, but Henry remembered.

Grace has been very good about keeping in touch and calls me a couple times a week, often when she is driving between appointments. I am always grateful for her attentions. We can talk for hours when we have the time. If she is not driving, we talk as we cook dinner and sometimes continue talking as we eat dinner. Sometimes she says, "Mom, can you wait a minute. I need to pay for this," as she grocery shops or picks up take-out food. Eventually, we agree we need to get off the phone and do something productive. However, she is definitely doing something valuable for me.

Henry and I don't talk often, partly because of the time difference between the east and west coasts. By the time he is finishing work, I am going to bed. When I asked him retrospectively what his feelings were about his father's death, he reminded me that they would be different from mine. He didn't have the same daily reminders that I did that his father was gone. He felt I had been dealt a major blow and I needed to figure out how to proceed. He wondered if I would keep busy enough. He didn't think I was depressed. Apparently, I fooled him like many others. He also wondered if I would go off the rails and he would have to change his level of emotional support. I always detected a sense of relief when I chattered away on the phone about all the exciting things I was doing and the interesting people I was meeting.

Parents and their children grieve differently over the loss of a family member. I never knew exactly what Henry and Grace were thinking. I am very grateful to have had their support, in different ways. They are completely different personalities and have different perspectives to offer. I like that and am very fortunate to have them both.

looking for depth

When John and I lived in Boston, we belonged to one of our Quaker meeting's spiritual growth groups. We were a group of eight or so—a neuroscientist, a music therapist, a membership director, two social workers, a higher ed student life administrator, John, and me. These folks became some of our closest friends. We were all very open to different ways of seeing God or Spirit in our lives and in others. We met in someone's home each month, and our host or hostess came up with a topic for us to discuss, anything from how we celebrated Christmas to what steps we were going to take to rectify racism. I found our deep sharing tremendously satisfying. Leaving this community behind when I left Boston was a huge loss.

John and I lived in North Carolina for four years before he died. We had tried to replicate our Boston spiritual experience by attending a similar Quaker meeting in North Carolina. After a year or so, we realized that this wasn't filling our need for connection. It was difficult to replace our experience and the relationships we had built over twenty-five years in Boston.

One day John said, "I'm not getting anything out of going to meeting. I'm staying home." He was faster at evaluating things than I was, but I realized I felt the same. We stopped attending, and for the first time in years, we had the experience of staying home on Sunday mornings, a quiet time with no obligations. We had no need to rush off in the morning to spend most of the day in worship and a committee meeting. I was disappointed that I hadn't found another faith community where deep sharing might be possible, but I still had John.

When I lost John, I lost my best friend, someone with whom I shared deeply and honestly. I missed this. The longer I lived by myself, the more I craved this depth of sharing. I needed another spiritual home.

I tried attending other Quaker meetings in the area, knowing that each one had a different personality. Nothing seemed right. I felt like Goldilocks: this one was too church-like, that one was too casual, or this one was too rigid. I spent my Sunday mornings alone, doing chores or cleaning the house. I continued to yearn for the depth of sharing I had experienced with my spiritual growth group in Boston. I was determined to successfully remake my life, so I considered starting my own spirituality group in the fall after John died in 2016.

I had a few possible candidates in mind, my neighbors Tad and Mary whom I was told were Quakers and a woman in my village who attended one of the local meetings. While out walking one day, I saw Tad walking his two Welsh terriers. I approached him while he tried to keep one of the dogs from lunging at me.

Over the barking I said, "Hi, I'm Linda Patterson. I live down the street and met you and your wife at Jan and Mark's. I am thinking about starting a small spiritual growth group with Quakers in the area. I remember that you guys are Quakers."

"Oh, uh, no, we're not Quakers," he said. "We just attended a Quaker meeting for six or seven years when we lived in New Jersey."

"Ah, okay," I said and continued on my walk. Clearly, he wasn't interested. Sometime later I received a call from his wife Mary, who said, "Tad told me you mentioned something about starting a spirituality group. I might be interested. I have a degree in spirituality."

I invited her over to chat. She arrived with her head covered in a scarf. She mentioned that she had breast cancer, was undergoing chemo, and that it was going well. Her tumor was shrinking, and she was considering surgery the following spring. I made a mental note not to talk too much about my husband who had just died of cancer. Usually, cancer discussions are very uncomfortable for me, but she seemed to have good news, so I was happy for her. We talked about our religious backgrounds; hers was Catholic despite the hiatus in a Quaker meeting, while I had spent more than thirty years as a Quaker after being raised Presbyterian. We liked the idea of exploring spirituality from a variety of angles and looked forward to recruiting our friends and neighbors for our group. When Mary returned home, she emailed me and suggested we make our group all women. We planned to recruit during the fall and start holding meetings in early January. We continued to plan by email even when she was in the hospital briefly. She returned home and then was back in the hospital. I asked if she wanted me to take her husband Tad a meal or food. She said that would be helpful. I dropped off a casserole and some muffins, and Tad updated me occasionally on Mary's progress in the hospital. A virus decimated her lungs and left her on a respirator. Much to everyone's sadness, Mary died right before Christmas.

I wasn't sure my hoped-for spirituality group would get off the ground. Mary and I had recruited friends during the fall and had a group of about eight. However, I wasn't sure I wanted to lead the group alone. Knowing Mary would co-lead the group made me feel secure going forward. Going it alone was riskier.

While out to dinner with two friends, I mentioned my nascent group and both women were interested. In fact, Suz was an ordained interfaith minister. She was interested in leading the group with me. Hallelujah! We were off and running.

At our first meeting, everyone shared their faith background, and we had a wonderful mix of people, some who no longer practiced their faith and others who attended religious services regularly.

Suz and I developed a preliminary list of discussion topics to see what the group wanted to pursue. I proposed using the worship-sharing model of discussion I was familiar with as a Quaker. Worship-sharing requires participants to take turns and stay silent until each person has a chance to share their thoughts on the topic. The first year was a bit rocky as it took a while for people to feel comfortable with this method. Our members were so engaged they wanted to interrupt with questions, make suggestions, and randomly comment. Suz and I needed to gently remind our members to hold their remarks until each person had a chance to speak. The group also looked for a strong leader to guide it. As a Quaker from an unprogrammed meeting where no one led the service, I expected us all to share the responsibility of suggesting and leading topics. But during the first year, no one volunteered to lead a discussion. It took time to build trust, and eventually each person felt comfortable suggesting topics, leading the group, and staying silent long enough to give everyone space to speak.

The group's format has morphed over the years, but I had one rule that I held firm: no talk about politics. Our group started while Trump was president and most of us had strong feelings about him. I didn't want our sacred time to devolve into a political discussion or tirade.

Some of the women wanted to socialize, and the strict format was a bit confining for them. One member suggested a group lunch, so we started enjoying new restaurants together. I was looking for company on a movie night, so some of us started going out to the movies. During the years of the pandemic, we were a great source of support for each other. To deal with the isolation, we met every two weeks on

Zoom instead of once a month. We were there for each other whether one of us went through a crisis or got a new puppy.

We live in a friendly village and meet lots of people, but rarely have the occasion to develop those relationships on a deeper level. The women in my spirituality group have committed to sharing their thoughts and feelings in a group they have come to trust. We talk about our ups and downs in confidence and find reassurance knowing that we are not alone in our feelings. I am very grateful to have had these women in my life, particularly as I made my way as a new widow. I found the depth of sharing I craved.

finding support

When I first approached Tad in our neighborhood about joining a spiritual growth group, I had no idea that we would become good friends soon after his wife's death. Although it is unusual to have a male friend without a romantic attachment, I was in no shape to pursue a love interest a few months after John's death. I wanted to meet interesting people and create a network of supportive friends.

There were three of us in my neighborhood who had lost our spouses within a span of five months. John died at the end of July 2016; Tad's wife died mid-December; and his next-door neighbor Nancy had lost her husband in early August, four days after I lost John. She had endured eleven years before he succumbed to Alzheimer's disease. Six months later, she became a member of my women's spirituality group.

Tad loved to cook and threw marvelous dinner parties. I was pleased to be invited along with Nancy, Tad's son and daughter-in-law, and sometimes a couple of other people. By the time he plated dinner, his kitchen looked like a whirlwind had hit it, with cupboard doors open and pots and pans covering every surface. Nancy and I subtly closed the doors as we hung out in the kitchen chatting with Tad. He enjoyed cooking with unusual spices, so the smells were as tempting as the food, which was always delicious.

Other times Tad invited us to come to African drumming events. He had studied the djembe for years and enjoyed playing with a local group of men and women who sat around outdoors on warm evenings and beat out enticing rhythms. Sometimes there were dancers too. One evening Tad brought his drums to my house and tried to get me to mimic the beats he tapped out, but I could only limp along with my boney fingers and challenged sense of rhythm. I was surprised that he expected me to pick up the art on a first try.

Besides having the loss of our spouses in common, Tad and I were both interested in learning Spanish. I had a trip to Argentina planned, and Tad had some Spanish-speaking relatives that he wanted to be able to converse with more easily during family events. He had a facility for language and a phenomenal memory. He wanted us to practice our smattering of Spanish by memorizing plays. Yikes, that would have taken me a long time to do. I was still struggling with Spanish vocabulary. Instead, we went to a full-day Spanish language-immersion workshop. I didn't understand most of what was said, but excelled at all the art projects. Tad understood more than I did but was totally frustrated by the hands-on activities. We all have our strengths, so I decided the best way for me to learn Spanish was to join a traditional weekly class. Tad learned on his own.

Tad was enamored with poetry. When he mentioned the poems he and his wife Mary recited at their wedding, I didn't recognize any of the titles. Emily Dickinson was his favorite poet, and he could recite her poems from memory. I used to tease him that he had an Emily Dickinson poem for every occasion.

There was one evening when he wanted to share Emily's poetry with me. He arrived at my house, poetry book in hand. After he cooked an elaborate dinner in my kitchen, complete with a whole fish whose staring eye gave me the creeps, we retired to the living room. He sat in a recliner as I sat on the couch across the room. He read a poem and asked me what I thought it meant. I hadn't a clue. I couldn't remember the lines from the beginning to the end of the poem. Analyzing poetry had never been my forte. He kindly read each line and paused, waiting for my analysis. This didn't help. I was getting embarrassed. I told him I couldn't remember the lines. He brought the book over so I could read them myself. He retreated to his chair. I read the poem to myself and, at his prompting, read each line out loud. This didn't help either. I still didn't know what the poem meant. He finally interpreted it for me. Good thing. I never would have guessed the meaning.

Despite our differences in style, our friendship endured. I tend to do best one-on-one and was delighted to have a new friend, especially because friendships with men are so rare. In the spring, Tad told me about an ongoing weekly bereavement group he had started attending. A fellow golfer, also a recent widower, had told Tad about it as they walked the golf course. I went with him one Tuesday afternoon. The group of thirty or forty people met in a church fellowship hall. We sat on plastic folding chairs at round tables where we were treated to cookies and coffee during the pre-program social hour. During the program, we moved to chairs arranged in a semi-circle around a podium. The convener welcomed newcomers and reminded attendees of the rules, primarily listening without offering people suggestions and the importance of maintaining confidentiality. Then he introduced the week's speaker, who presented for twenty to thirty minutes on a topic related to grieving. After the presentation we were divided up into discussion groups of about ten people and went to different rooms in the church. There were two facilitators for each group who kept the conversation going and made sure no one dominated the discussion.

At my first meeting, we introduced ourselves and identified whom we had lost and how long ago. I saw a mass of very sad people. The entire experience was distressing, but I came back week after week. This group offered me a place to be with people who were as sad as I was and who understood my feelings.

The group was very diverse: people from all walks of life who had lost their spouses, partners, parents, grandparents, children, or siblings. Some people had multiple losses in a short period of time. I listened carefully to everyone's story and found the different perspectives fascinating. This ongoing drop-in group was exactly what I needed. It offered me the camaraderie of people who were also finding their ways in the midst of grief. I was always quick to share my grief with the group, and although I don't remember this, a friend from the group said I cried every week.

I remember one discussion group in particular. I had read in the rules that this was not a place to mourn pets. I don't think many other people knew this rule. As my small discussion group waited for our facilitators to join us, a woman said she was there because her dog had died. Despite our diverse losses, the death of a pet was something we all could relate to. We were riveted as we consoled this woman and shared our own pet loss stories. We may not have been following the rules, but it was one of the most meaningful discussions I had there.

Tad and I carpooled to this group most weeks. It was nice to have someone to talk to during the thirty-minute drive. One of the notable things he said during this time was, "This isn't going away." It may sound obvious, but to a grieving person who is hoping the nightmare will end, this is a revelation.

Close to the anniversary of John's death, a man in the bereavement group stopped me after our session and said that the anniversary of his wife's death was a turning point for him, so I should expect some relief. I thanked him, started to cry, and he gave me a hug. I went to the ladies' room, hid in a stall, and sobbed. In the car, I told Tad that I didn't know why I was sad. All the other people at the bereavement group had sorrow too. I had a good life, a nice house, food to eat. Tad looked straight ahead, hands on the steering wheel, and said, "You know why you are sad. Stop feeling guilty about it."

After the bereavement group, Tad and I usually stopped for dinner at a restaurant on the way home to rehash the topic of the afternoon. As we got to know people in the group, we invited them to come to dinner with us. Soon we had a regular group of seven or eight people who relished the opportunity to share a meal since they were not going home to anyone. The sharing at the bereavement discussion groups was satisfying, but our dinner discussions were livelier and deeper in this small, consistent group. We developed a special closeness.

One night, one of the women in the group asked us to come to her house to help her hand out Halloween candy, a favorite tradition. Another time, we went to a Christmas tree lighting event, and still another evening, I had everyone come to my house for a potluck dinner. The group even went to a jazz club on some evenings. Charlie, one of our members, loved to dance, as do I. Tad was uncomfortable dancing, so Charlie and I were always the first on the dance floor. Eventually others in our group danced. Charlie was such a good dancer that patrons would stop him as he left the club to remark on his skill. Considering that Charlie was in his late eighties and as thin as a rail, he cut a memorable figure.

The closeness of this group lasted for many months, until the group started to expand and we lost our intimacy. A year after I started attending the bereavement group, I spent the summer in Boston rekindling old friendships and spending time with my daughter. When I returned in September, our dinner group was eating at Chick-Fil-A regularly and enlisted Charlie, a retired pastor, to say grace in the restaurant. Neither Tad nor I were enthusiastic about fast food and slowly drifted away from the group in the fall.

Before I left for Boston, Tad and I were at a restaurant with some of our dinner group. His behavior was unusual that evening. He stared intently at one of the women across the table. Then he would be busy texting in his lap. When we all left, I caught Tad outside. We had come in separate cars that evening. I said, "What's going on? You seem different tonight."

Tad said, "Nothing. I'm just distracted. I am taking a friend to the airport tomorrow, and we were texting to make plans."

"Oh, okay. See you later." I dismissed my concern and drove home. After I was home for an hour or so, the phone rang. It was Tad.

"You are so perceptive. Something is different. I was introduced to this incredible woman at lunch on Sunday, and I knew then that everything had changed."

Tad then proceeded to tell me that her name was Mary, like his late wife's, and that she had a divinity degree from

Harvard University. Tad had gone to Harvard, and his late wife had a degree in spirituality. The new Mary had worked for a United Nations development agency in West Africa. Tad had worked for the Peace Corps in neighboring Nigeria. The commonalities were amazing, and they were married the next spring. It was like a fairy tale romance. I have heard many times that widowed men remarry faster than widowed women. I was very happy for him. Mary lived in our village, so when she and Tad bought a house together, they stayed in the village. Mary was such a wonderful, inclusive person that when they married, I didn't lose Tad as a friend, but gained another in Mary.

looking for myself

John and I were married when I was thirty. For the next thirty-six years we were a team. My model for living was as part of a couple. When I was widowed, I wasn't exactly sure who I was as an individual. It was like learning to stand and balance on one leg. I had to strengthen a lot of muscles I hadn't used for a while. I needed to find my center and develop a new strategy.

Forging ahead by myself was scary. To protect myself from fear and sadness, I walled myself off from missing John by thinking about how different and exciting my future would be. It was almost as if I was a child railing against a parent and saying, "When I grow up things will be different." I focused on opportunities I would have as a single person. My friend Carole told me recently that my friends could see the sadness written on my face and body even though I thought I was being brave.

I spent my first year of bereavement trying to separate myself from John. Where did John end and I begin? I pondered this a lot after he died. Had the line between us blurred too much? Had I allowed John to change me? Did I need to reclaim myself? It was almost as if I had to prove myself to myself.

John and I had influenced each other's lives profoundly, but at first, I couldn't identify the specific ways we each had been changed. The blend that was us clouded those specifics. I was also somewhat defensive because I don't like to feel I am ever under the influence of other people. There was such a mix of emotions, many of which I didn't identify until much later. At one level, I felt hopeful for the future, but on a deeper level I felt abandoned and vulnerable. I didn't want to admit that I had lost something so important.

When John and I first got together, he was very liberal and relaxed. I was uptight and followed the rules. As the years went by, I mellowed, and he tightened up. Our puzzle pieces began to fit together. Where I had gaps in my knowledge, he had the answers. He liked to build things, I liked to refinish and paint. If I was too lax with our children, he kept a tight rein. If one of them didn't hold their fork correctly, he noticed. I was too busy eating.

In one session of my drop-in bereavement group, the presenter talked about holding a lost loved one's behavior in our bodies. I experienced this with my mother's death by developing a yen for her favorite foods long after she died. After John died, I unintentionally mimicked some of his behaviors too. John never allowed us to watch TV in a darkened room, so to this day, I turn on a light while watching TV. For thirty-six years, he insisted that we stay until the very end of a movie's credits. I never figured out why the credits were so important to him, but it has taken me a while to break this habit. John didn't like knives in the dish drainer, so I was careful to put them away after washing them. He insisted we eat crunchy peanut butter. I still eat crunchy peanut butter. I now drink his favorite tea. And I still leave the heel of the bread on the end of the loaf to keep the rest of the bread fresh because John did this.

When I became aware of blindly following his preferences years after his death, I joked to myself that I should have made a list of John's rules. It rankled me that following his preferences was so ingrained. I almost felt resentful that he held such sway over me in death. I never felt that way when he was alive. I always felt like he was easy-going and tolerant. With all these implanted behaviors, how would I ever move on and find my true essence?

After his death, I drew the line at some of his habits. He had a rigid schedule and was in front of the television every night at six p.m. to watch *PBS News Hour.* I only watched occasionally. However, when I heard the announcement that Gwen Ifill, a favorite newscaster on the show, had died, I pounded my fist and screamed, "No, no, no!" It was another loss that I associated with John. After the news each night, he watched *Jeopardy!* He loved *Jeopardy!* I hated it. I couldn't answer most of the questions and it made me feel stupid. I would have preferred to watch the business news. I have never watched *Jeopardy!* since John died.

Many cultures prescribe a specific mourning period. I assumed from this that grief was finite, like an illness or injury. I thought I would take a year to heal and then move on. A retired doctor warned that it would take three years, but that was unfathomable. In the first year of my grief, I protected myself from sadness by not thinking about my happiest memories with John. We both loved theater and pursued it, he in community theater and I in a small local opera chorus. We both enjoyed humor and art. One evening, I called my son to talk. During the conversation, I admitted that I had been feeling sad. I mentioned one of Henry's friends from first grade who had come for dinner one night. This little boy was surprised at how affectionate John and I were. When I reminded him of that, Henry told me, "You guys were not the usual parents—you were always singing and being theatrical." I had forgotten this side of us.

The next morning, I spoke with my daughter and asked about her recollections of John and me as parents. Grace said, "You were goofy, but in a good way. My friend Leah said you were perfect together. You were outgoing and really put yourselves out there." Being reminded of these precious memories helped me feel more in touch with what I had lost. I had filtered out the happy memories too painful to recall. I wasn't ready to face my loss. My conscious mind kept a grip on when to open the door to happier reflections.

After talking to Grace, I sat at my desk wincing in pain, the tears streaming down my face. I felt like my loss was coming into focus. As I cried, my cat Riley lay on my desk, looking at me. I know he felt the change when John died, but he had moved on in his life. He was aware of John's illness, watched John die, took it all in, adjusted to the change, and was now living his new circumstances. I wish it was that easy for me. I had to slog through layers and phases of grief with more to come.

The first twelve months had initially offered the distraction of busyness, a miscalculated hope for the future, and eventually the recognition of my loss. It took a year before I could see that my emerging self had been built from layers and layers of experience since the day I was born. I had not lost part of myself because I had adopted some of John's ideas. They had added to my ever-evolving self. And I know that I changed John as much as he changed me.

I finally accepted that partnering with John changed my life. But it would take years before I felt comfortable enough with myself to look at some of John's rules with fondness. Now, after washing the sharp knives, sometimes I dry them and put them away and sometimes I leave them in the dish drainer. It's my choice. But my desire to be magically released after a year of grief faded because I knew there was a long way to go.

shifting values

Death has a way of changing one's perspective. In one of the bereavement groups I attended, a presenter suggested that we became different people as soon as we lost a loved one. I railed at the thought. I am not a different person just because John died. I may need to develop unused aspects of my personality, but I am the same person. The truth is that even before John died, we were changing as we accepted inevitable loss.

John had grown up in a household where finances were tight, and his adult attitudes about money reflected this. I had grown up in a financially secure family, but my father had experienced hard times as a child. He was very careful and secretive about money. We never discussed finances. After a day of shopping for bargains with my mother when I was small, I asked her, "Are we poor?" She reassured me that we were not, but I retained the message that saving money was paramount. As a result of our childhood experiences, both John and I were very frugal.

On dates, we used to count out pennies when we split the restaurant bill. As a young married couple, we were so money conscious we used to create quarterly reports based on our annual budget. I clipped coupons, much to my children's chagrin. They were always exasperated when I pulled out my coupons in a restaurant and told them what they should order to save money. It was reminiscent of my childhood when my father always suggested that I order chicken because it was the cheapest thing on the menu. Grace picked up on our attitudes as a small child and, like an echo from the past, asked me, "Are we poor?"

"No," I said, "we're not poor, just very thrifty."

My mother died suddenly from undiagnosed colon cancer when John and I were in our late forties. The speed with which life can be lost made a big impression on him and affected his attitude about money. We had planned a trip to Disney World. I diligently researched budget hotels in Orlando until John said, "If we are going to Disney World, we are going to stay in the park. This will probably be the only time we do this, and we should do it right." I was shocked. This was not the man I married.

At Disney World we stayed at the Polynesian Hotel and had no regrets. That was the only time we went to Disney World, but we didn't shrink from trips to Africa for our twenty-fifth wedding anniversary and to Korea when Grace graduated from college. I treasure these travel memories to this day.

When we were told John would only live a year, I called our financial planner. We had just finished making adjustments to our Social Security benefits based on scenarios where we would live long lives. This new, sad information meant our planner needed to run other scenarios. Alone, I pulled into a parking lot away from home and called him with the news and the new request. I wasn't ready to tell John I was attending to this practical detail. His style may have been to open up to family before getting all the facts, but I approached critical decisions more privately.

When the planner sent a new financial tack, I told John about my conversation. We contacted the Social Security Administration and changed how we took our benefits.

This ushered in a new way of looking at life or what was left of it. I still saved coupons, but I also felt like time was limited and I wanted John to have whatever he desired. I decided I should have whatever I wanted too. We both needed to make the most of whatever time was left. While John lay in bed, I went out shopping. He had never liked our living room coffee table, and I spotted a unique one with an inlaid design at an estate sale down the street. I snapped a picture of it and sent it to him. He said to go ahead and buy it. I had always wanted hand-thrown clay dinner plates, but they are very expensive, so I never bought any. Again, John said to buy them from our favorite potter. I did.

A few months earlier, I had cleaned up the yard and crawl space and now took a hard look at the interior of our house. I imagined it would feel a little big for one person. I liked cozy spaces and dreaded rattling around in an empty house after John died. I was imagining how lonely I would feel. I kept telling myself that I would just have to "live large" to fill the space. Unconvinced I would feel up to living large, I hired painters and had all the white walls painted a pale gray or cream to make the space seem smaller. It was a good idea. The color made the environment warmer.

I also decided to move our office from the end of the house to the guest room, which was closer to the living room. This gave the living space a more compact feel. However, I was moving our office into a smaller space. The original office had a walk-in closet where we kept two large file cabinets. I shredded stacks of paper statements and only kept digital copies to conserve space. John was skeptical and guarded his financial statements from my shredder. I also whittled down office resources—copier paper, binders, briefcases, and blank DVDs—and managed to wedge the survivors, along with a four-drawer file cabinet, into the small closet in the new office. While John was feeling relatively well, he helped me push desks into position and move beds. We both liked the new, smaller office space. It gave us a clear view of anyone coming down the driveway or walking up to the house.

Two years before John's death, I had surgery on my right ankle. It took months for me to fully recover, so John did most of the housework himself. I felt guilty seeing him spend hours every Saturday cleaning the house. When I suggested he hire someone to help, he said, "As long as I can do this, I am going to do it." To him, it was an unnecessary expense to hire someone if he could do the cleaning. I used my knee scooter to move about the house to dust and do what I could. Unfortunately, by pushing my limits on the scooter, I tore the meniscus in my left knee, an injury that plagued me for years.

While John was sick, I struggled to keep up with house cleaning along with my nursing duties. We had always shared the work, but my bad knee made it difficult to stoop down and clean under toilets and furniture. Finally, I said, "John, I can't do all the housework myself. I want to hire someone to help." He was all for it. I hired a couple of women to clean once a week. After he died, I kept them on.

Our financial planner told me I didn't need to clip coupons anymore. This was not an easy mindset to change. I had been brought up to scrimp and save. I tasted this new life by going out to eat more often. I needed the socialization, so I was able to justify the expense. Eventually, I stopped looking for the cheapest thing on the menu and bought whatever I wanted. After all, since John was gone, I had more money to spend and could eat for two. I learned to eat out and not feel guilty.

John had been very generous, but I maintained my frugal ways even when considering charities. John had experienced hunger as a teenager and young adult, so he was particularly supportive of food pantries and food banks. Once I started spending more freely, I felt more comfortable following his example. My financial planner reassured me that I would not run out of money unless I became extravagant.

My shopping habits changed too. I realized that I was spending too much time in grocery stores comparing prices and not always buying what I wanted. What was I saving my money for? One day while shopping for toilet paper, it occurred to me that I could buy any kind I wanted. John and I had bought the same toilet paper for thirty-five years because it was the most economical. I didn't need to do that anymore. I may not have needed to do that while we were married either, but we never considered it. I pushed my cart along the tall row of toilet paper brands, squeezing rolls and reading labels. I pondered two-ply and patterns and considered the number of sheets in each roll. I finally picked out a jumbo package and reassured myself that if I didn't like this kind, I could buy another type next month. This was a true revelation.

After I chose toilet paper, I realized I could buy all sorts of things that I had always wanted, but John had vetoed. There was a true liberation about making decisions without compromising with a partner. I bought pre-moistened towelettes for quick clean-ups. John thought they were wasteful. I tried new paper towels, new cat litter, new cat food, and stocked up on pickled beets, one of my favorite foods. The sky was the limit. I was going to enjoy life.

the first holidays

The first year of my bereavement, I planned something special for each holiday or important date so I wouldn't dwell on John's absence. He died at the end of July 2016, and I held his North Carolina memorial service in August and his Boston memorial service in September. At the end of October, I viewed the extraordinary local pumpkin carving displays in my village with the other souls wandering in the dark, but in November, I planned to avoid Thanksgiving gatherings.

Thanksgiving has always been one of my favorite holidays. When our children were young, we often ate with a large group at our Quaker meeting, but in more recent years John and I had Thanksgiving alone and our children dined with their friends. Not having Thanksgiving with John this year was too painful to think about, so I made other plans. I didn't want to be appended to anyone's family nor did I want to be folded into a group. I love train trips and museums, so I took the train to Washington, DC, by myself.

In Washington, I spent Thanksgiving Day and Friday wandering through the National Museum of the American Indian and the National Portrait Gallery and taking in a movie at the National Air and Space Museum. The one part of the holiday I didn't want to give up was the turkey, mashed potatoes, and cranberry sauce, which has always been one of my favorite meals.

On Thanksgiving Day at the museum cafeteria, I had the traditional meal for lunch and then made a reservation for Thanksgiving dinner at a nice restaurant. That evening I was ushered to a small corner table with a white tablecloth surrounded by the warmth of old mahogany paneling. Eating by myself in a restaurant was lonely, but at least I was adjacent to other quiet diners. These strangers expected no upbeat conversation from me, no smiles, no false composure that a group of my peers or family might have expected. To my surprise, the restaurant had a piano and cello combo playing jazz standards. I was delighted. I was so enthralled with the entertainment that I thought it was good John wasn't there, for I would have been ignoring him.

At Christmas, Grace, Henry, Henry's boyfriend Keith, and I met in San Diego, where I had rented a beachfront condo for a week. If you stood in front of the window and leaned to the right, you could see the Pacific Ocean. We had a wonderful time walking on the beaches, taking a brewery tour, and visiting the famous zoo. It was a very pleasant week despite Grace losing her iPhone and getting a traffic ticket on Christmas Eve because I gave her bad driving directions.

The most important part was that I was with my children. This was the only time of year I got to see Henry and Grace together. We had a tiny family, but I treasured it. Before we left, Henry gave me a card with a note inside:

Dear Mommy,

Merry Christmas and what a year!

Although I can't help but be worried about you after losing Daddy, I was impressed even toward the end of his illness with how many ideas you had about ways to pursue your interests in the future. This has been a continuing theme ever since you moved to NC—you've found new and exciting ways to spend your time even in the face of not having a full-time job (and now, a companion). I'm excited to see you travel more (and to join you on some of those trips), volunteer for more causes, and show Grace, me, and everyone around you that leading an interesting life is a habit, not a static state. Speaking of Grace, I'm very glad for all kinds of reasons, both logistical and emotional, she was able to be closer to you during Daddy's illness than I was. Even though I played a much more disconnected part, I want to let you know that if you need anything, I'm always here—especially if you're feeling less bullish and secure about your future than it seems from the outside. I'll be there when it counts.

I don't say it often, but I love you.

– Henry

I was very touched. This note is a treasure from a son who usually keeps his feelings under wraps.

Back in North Carolina, I signed up for a New Year's Day walk in the woods led by a nature conservation organization on one of their properties. John had been a donor, and I thought participating in one of their treks would be a good way to learn about the organization. I was delighted to find that I knew the director, who was also on the hike. Otherwise, I would have been very lonely trailing behind a group of strangers. Just because I was being brave to venture out by myself didn't mean that I wasn't gritting my teeth at times. Carrying on alone is not easy.

John and I both had February birthdays a few days apart that often fell during the long Presidents' Day weekend. We celebrated with ski trips or short jaunts and made more of a fuss on our birthdays than on our wedding anniversary. In fact, we forgot our first wedding anniversary until a friend called to congratulate me. Our birthdays were so important to us that we had wedding rings designed with wide strips of amethyst, the birthstone for February. When we lived in Boston, we had friends who had birthdays on the same days as ours, so the group of us would go to an IMAX movie at the Museum of Science and then out to dinner. It was such fun. I had no prospects for celebrating my birthday the first year after John died, but Grace was kind enough to fly to North

Carolina and spend the birthday week with me. I folded her into my appointment with my financial planner, my swim class, dinner with friends, a concert, and a special dinner for my birthday. We did not dwell on John. She knew I was working hard to not wallow in the mire of sadness.

John and I had always said we would go to the Outer Banks sometime, but never made it. He was a redhead and sunburned easily, so he was not highly motivated to spend time in the sun. In February, soon after John's diagnosis, I mentioned a trip to the Outer Banks to Grace, but it never happened. John never felt up to it. The trip was still on my bucket list, so I rented a beachfront condo on the Outer Banks in June and Grace, Grace's boyfriend Charles, and I enjoyed a week at the shore. The first time I met Charles was when I picked them up at the airport. He was a warm and friendly guy who gave me a hug at the airport and later cooked me the best scallops I have had in my life.

A year had almost passed. I had successfully made it through major holidays, but I had one more important date to weather, John's death anniversary.

death anniversary

The last day and night of John's life was seared into my memory. Grace, John's cousin Faye, and I worked as a team, and we each brought something to his care. Faye is a thoughtful person and a calming presence. Grace is also very thoughtful and sensitive. She had been my constant companion during this strenuous time, and I relied on her to be the voice of reason and to remind me of things I overlooked. I treasured their presence at this memorable event, and I wanted to commemorate the closeness I felt with them.

Faye had made two trips to North Carolina while John was ill, so I decided Grace and I would go to Davis, California, where Faye lived. Our group expanded to six because Faye's daughter Amber lived nearby, and Henry and Keith lived about ninety minutes away in San Francisco. I rented a lovely three-bedroom home, sight unseen, outside of Lassen Volcanic National Park for our mini-reunion.

Grace and I spent a few days at Amber's home before the four of us headed to the national park for the weekend. I timed our visit to coincide with John's death date on a Sunday that year. We arrived at the rented house on Friday afternoon; Henry and Keith arrived that evening. John was always top of mind for me, and I frequently mentioned him. I expected that we would sit around and share stories about John during the weekend, but that is not what happened.

Saturday morning, we packed a lunch and headed off to the national park. We hiked a variety of trails, saw waterfalls, picnicked, and spent a lovely day kayaking on a lake. We had driven two cars to the park, so I rode back to the house with Henry and Keith.

"So, Henry, do you have any special memories about your father?" I asked.

"I haven't had much of a relationship with him for years. I will have to think about it," he said.

I wanted to snap back, "That's because you left home at age fifteen to go to boarding school." But I bit my tongue, not wanting to revisit my anger that he left home so young. Going to boarding school had been his idea.

That evening we put dinner together from the food we all brought and shared a congenial meal as the cousins continued getting to know each other. Amber was about ten years older than Henry and had last met Grace when Grace was a teenager. Despite the pleasant conversation, there were still no stories about John. I was a little perplexed and saddened, but happy we were all together.

Sunday morning, Henry and I were in the kitchen alone fixing our breakfasts. As I buttered toast, I mentioned that today was the anniversary of his father's death. Henry said, "Oh, is this the exact day?" My eyes widened. I was flabbergasted. When I recall the scene now, I fantasize stamping my foot and screaming at him in response, but I only smiled benignly and said, "Yes, it is."

Amber was a professor and needed to work most of the weekend, so she sat on the porch or in the yard with her laptop enjoying the sunny weather. Faye spent most of her time sitting next to Amber and reading. She had been so present when she visited us in North Carolina, but now she seemed so quiet. I was concerned, but Amber assured me her mother was fine.

Fortunately, my friends from home were attentive. I received six email messages remembering John's death anniversary during the weekend. However, everyone in the house seemed to be on a different wavelength than I was. Henry seemed oblivious to why he and Keith were there.

After they drove back to San Francisco on Sunday, and as Faye and Amber were reading in the sun, I was bewildered and vented my frustration to Grace as she lounged on the couch, "Do you have a special memory of your dad?"

She paused and said, "I couldn't pick just one. I have so many."

Sunday evening with just the four of us, I decided to be more direct about what I wanted.

"Faye and Amber, do you have any special memories of John?" Amber got a pass since she wouldn't have spent much time with him as an adult. Faye thought about my question for a while and recalled John and her ex-husband doing Monty Python silly walks when the three of them hiked in the Rocky Mountains. I was grateful that she could come up with something. I treasure any memory of John that people share with me.

Sometime later, Faye told me that she was aware of my reason for bringing us together, but the house in California didn't remind her of John. She had known him in a completely different context. I guess that was the problem; we all had our perspectives. I couldn't expect anyone else to miss John like I was missing him. He had been a part of my daily life, and his last night alive may have been a poignant memory for me, but not so for the others, especially those who were not there.

After my friend Tad remarried, his new wife Mary gave a dinner party in memory of his first wife. A few close friends attended, in addition to Tad's son and his wife. I wondered if this get-together would go any better than my own family gathering on John's death anniversary. At Tad and Mary's, I listened to the chitchat as we sampled appetizers in the living room. I sat quietly after we were called to the dinner table and made more small talk. Finally, I was so anxious that no one would mention Tad's late wife, I recounted my own family's story to prompt the diners to share their memories. That broke the ice, and the stories poured forth. I was greatly relieved. To have sat there without hearing memories of Tad's first wife, the reason we were having dinner together, would have been like reliving the silence of John's death anniversary.

Ever since John died, I have talked about him and told our stories as much as I did when he was alive. This keeps him present for me and reminds me how fortunate I have been. Many of my current friends did not know him or did not know him well. He was a quiet guy. Just as our wedding anniversary was not the most important day of the year for us, I don't dwell on his death anniversary. It is not the only day to celebrate him. Every day is.

massaging christmas

Of all the holidays, Christmas is the one I now look forward to the most because I get to see my children. The holiday morphed over the years since the birth of our son Henry and continues to evolve. We have shaped and massaged it to fit our ever-changing family.

We are a tiny family of three without John, and I am fortunate that my children have not been spirited off to their partners' homes for the holiday. Henry's partner is Jewish, but the mother of Grace's boyfriend took me aside one Thanksgiving and said, "Why don't you and Grace spend Christmas up here next year?" I explained that Henry and Grace were all the family I had, and I treasured our brief time together at Christmas. In fact, it is usually the only time I get to see my son all year. We do not have a traditional Christmas but put value on the simple act of being together. We had traditional Christmases when Grace and Henry were little, but as they grew, we found new ways to celebrate our time together.

My feelings about Christmas are complicated. As a child, I had a rich assortment of Christmas activities—singing in the junior choir at church, decorating the tree, giving and receiving gifts, and getting together with another family for Christmas dinner and board games afterward. As I grew, the magic started to disappear.

I only had one sibling, a brother who was five years my senior. When we were teenagers, our family no longer got together with the other family, a disappointment for me. I really enjoyed the games. When it was just the four of us, my mother started to prepare our midday dinner early Christmas morning and wanted gift opening done on her timeline. She preferred a free-for-all where everyone dove in at once and finished quickly. Every year it seemed she said, "Hurry up, hurry up. I need to get back to the kitchen."

I longed for a family who sat around and watched each other open gifts, one at a time, oohing and aahing over each newfound treasure or finding pleasure in giving the gift that delighted. What's Christmas if it is not a time to savor thoughtfulness and time together?

While my brother and I unwrapped our presents, my mother and father sneaked off to a corner, laughing at their inside jokes, and exchanged their gifts, usually hidden under the couch. In retrospect I should have appreciated that they still had a special relationship after all their years of marriage. At the time I just felt shut out.

Despite my disappointments with Christmas morning, I have some fun Christmas Eve memories as a young adult. Sometimes, when I was home from college, I would decorate the tree myself if my parents were out for the evening. My mother was always pleased. On Christmas Eve, she and I had an unconventional tradition of "clunking" the gifts, as John called it. We sat on the couch in the twilight of Christmas tree lights, shaking and palpating all the wrapped presents trying to guess what was inside. No one else indulged in this activity until I passed the tradition on to my children. In my mind, trying to guess what was inside was a fun detective game.

John was very accommodating to my family when we were first married. Every year at Christmas we drove the seven and a half hours from Boston through New York holiday traffic to my parents' house in Delaware. We have pictures of one-year-old Henry, the first grandchild, sitting amid piles of gifts taller than he was. This excess went on year after year. My parents had even more fun when our daughter Grace arrived.

Things were more complicated when Grace and Henry were a little older. My childhood family used to enjoy games, but now it was difficult to lure my dad out of his den. If we wanted to take Henry and Grace to an outdoor light show Christmas Eve, my mother was concerned about the timing of dinner, the cold, or the fact that my father was singing in church later that evening. We were a young family ready for adventure, and my parents were in their mid-seventies, ready to slow down.

Eventually, John and I created our own holiday traditions in our Massachusetts home and visited my parents in Delaware every other year. Our town offered a visit by Santa, who would bring our children gifts that we had secretly bought. And, on Christmas morning, we opened our gifts one at a time.

I have treasured memories of toddler Henry's squeal, "It's a Whamborgeenie!" when Santa brought him a coveted model car. But there was also the annual gift of clothing from my mother that he referred to as the dreaded clothing box. Four-year-old Grace tried on her gifts of clothing from my mother by laying them on the floor and lying on top of them.

My mother had been the center of holiday activities. She threw a dinner party a few days after Christmas each year for her two sisters and their families. My brother, two aunts and uncles, a few cousins, and their children attended. Not a big group. After my mother died, we never saw them again except at my parents' memorial services. John, Henry, Grace, and I were on our own for the holidays in Massachusetts. My dream of a large, affectionate family faded.

By the time Henry was fourteen and Grace eleven, both my parents had passed away. Our family had shrunk. Our Christmases became less eventful. Now, we only snapped a few badly lit pictures of the children opening their gifts.

Decorating the tree was always a production, one that I came to dislike. Henry and Grace usually went with John and me to pick out a tree. Back home, we put on Christmas music, sawed off the end of the trunk, and fitted the trunk into the stand. One parent would twirl the tree while the other assessed which side would look best in the front. John put the lights on the tree, I critiqued the placement, he rearranged them, and then we hung the ornaments. When Henry and Grace were very young, they were excited to help. However, we had to rearrange their placement of the heaviest balls on the weakest bottom branches or separate a clump of balls on one side of the tree to even it out. As they grew older, they lost interest and drifted off to their rooms. As the years went on, John and I were decorating the trees ourselves.

I grew up in the age of metal tinsel with strands that were very difficult to separate and hang gracefully on the tree. My father constantly admonished us not to throw the tinsel on the tree in clumps. As a result, he and my mother usually did most of the decorating too. I could identify with my parents' waning interest. In fact, John and I became resentful doing all the work ourselves. Just as my Christmas experience changed when I was a teenager, the holiday was changing as my children became teenagers.

As my enthusiasm for decorating faded, my belief in the Christmas story dimmed as well. From my research before directing my first Christmas pageant at my Quaker meeting, I found information refuting the idea that Jesus was born in December since it was too cold in Bethlehem for shepherds and their sheep to be in the fields. What's more, the census took place in September or October before cold weather made travel difficult. There are many interpretations of the Greek text suggesting where Jesus was born. At the time of his birth, families often brought their animals into the first floor of their homes at night to protect them from theft. If Mary and Joseph had hoped to stay with Joseph's family in one of the upper rooms, perhaps there was only room for them on the first floor, but it was not a stable.

Our family's faith was changing too. Christmas Eve, when we were leaving our candlelight service at the meetinghouse, I heard one of my children say, "I can't believe someone gave

109

a message about Jesus." Despite my shock at the remark, I realized that religious faith was not what moved my family at Christmastime. Perhaps we needed to rethink this.

One year, long after John and I were tired of decorating for Christmas, I floated the idea of not buying a tree, but instead buying an evergreen garland and draping it on the fireplace mantel with some favorite ornaments.

"No, you can't do that. We need a tree!" was the response from my children. Sigh. We bought a tree that year.

Another year, I decided a trip would be an appropriate way to celebrate Christmas with teenagers. That way, they would be captives and could not escape to their rooms. A few days before Christmas, we flew to Los Angeles and went to Disneyland. The next day, we drove to downtown L.A. where I got a great deal on an upscale hotel in the financial district. On Christmas Eve we took a cab to Olvera Street to witness Las Posadas, the Mexican reenactment of Mary and Joseph's search for lodging before Jesus' birth. These few blocks in L.A. are like a slice of old Mexico in the heart of the city. We did not buy gifts for each other that year; the trip was the gift.

Christmas morning, we awoke under sumptuous down comforters and dined on an elegant breakfast near a fountain in the hotel's restaurant. The rest of the trip, we drove up the California coast past spectacular scenery while Henry and Grace slept in the car, much to John's and my frustration.

We rented a cabin sheltered by redwoods and saw sea lions basking on the rocks. The trip ended in San Francisco, where we sat in a restaurant on New Year's Eve as it poured rain outside. The children were disappointed that we didn't have a more spectacular New Year's, but it had been a wonderful trip. And traveling was a great model for future years. Being home for the holidays didn't hold the allure for me it once did.

The following year, we were invited to Cousin Amber's December wedding in Colorado. A huge snowfall closed the airport so we couldn't attend. Instead, we flew directly to Phoenix, where we had planned to spend Christmas with John's mother and her husband. The highlight of the trip was our hot air balloon ride over the Arizona terrain.

I had hoped our exciting trips would break the spell of ever needing a Christmas tree again, but they did not. The next time we stayed at home for Christmas, Henry and Grace insisted we get a tree. I said, "I'm tired of doing this alone. If you want a tree, you guys need to buy and decorate it. I am happy to pay for it, but Daddy and I are not going to do all the work."

Henry and Grace coordinated their schedules one evening, picked up a tree, put it on top of the car, and drove it home. They hoisted the tree into the stand and left it in the middle of the living room. I would have preferred it not blocking the traffic pattern, but I didn't say a thing. Who uses a living room these days, anyhow? A week went by until Henry and Grace's schedules meshed again, and they affixed the lights and hung the decorations. They put the tree in its place, and it was done. So, we had a tree that year and many subsequent years, but the trees got smaller and smaller when I bought them.

The year John and I moved to North Carolina, we broke with tradition again. We missed Boston and all met in a Boston hotel. Henry was living in California by then but arrived early to spend time with his friend Lydia. I escaped decorating a house and tree, but when Lydia drove Henry to our hotel, she brought a small Christmas tree and cookies she and Henry had baked.

The next few years, we were at home for Christmas, but eight months before John died with no inkling he was sick, we decided to be closer to family and fly to California for a few days' visit with John's cousin Faye and her daughter Amber in Davis. After our visit, we drove to Mendocino on the coast, where we spent Christmas. This was my last Christmas with John. Unfortunately, he didn't feel well enough to go out for Christmas Eve dinner with us at an upscale vegan restaurant, one of the few eateries open the day before Christmas. I don't know if I associate the vegan restaurant with John's last Christmas or not, but I still don't enjoy vegan food.

After John's death I wanted to continue our newfound tradition of traveling and avoid decorating a tree. Traveling would help me forget that John was not with us and give me a new perspective on the Christmas holidays. It would also give me some traveling partners. When I lost John, I also lost the dream of traveling with him in retirement.

Christmas no longer meant what it did when I was younger. The excitement was gone. We were not religious. Gifts were impractical. Henry kept a minimum of possessions and Grace collected too many. I didn't want more stuff. And there was no large family to welcome warmly into our home. After years of resisting holiday trappings and pondering the best way to spend holiday family time, I concluded that experiencing someplace new together would be meaningful for the three of us.

For the first Christmas after John's death, we traveled to one of the places on my bucket list, San Diego. The following year Henry and I were of like mind and wanted to go to Buenos Aires, another place on my bucket list. Grace was happy to go anywhere warm. When Henry was a baby, we had a much-loved nanny from Argentina. She piqued our interest with the stories about her homeland. I had to make the trip without John but was grateful Henry and Grace wanted to go with me.

Traveling to Buenos Aires was a major undertaking, but I was lucky to rent a condo from a Canadian. I had taken Spanish lessons during the year but didn't realize that the Argentine accent would challenge my minimal language skills. Fortunately, Henry's Spanish was better than mine, so when we needed to purchase and install Argentine chips for our phones, Henry led the way. We had to learn the bus, the money, and the grocery store systems. And we had to be tolerant of each other's traveling styles. I am a planner, but Henry likes to explore a new city on foot without an itinerary. We often split up and I would tour a museum while Henry and Grace hiked the urban parks for hours. Sometimes they would walk the mile to a bookstore while I rode the bus to meet them. Or they went out clubbing while I went to bed.

Thankfully there was no decorating for Christmas, but I was happy to cook a traditional dinner with my favorite sides.

Instead of a turkey, we bought a whole chicken a couple of days before the twenty-fourth. It smelled a little off when I took it out of the bag to roast it Christmas Eve. Since all the stores and restaurants were closed and we would have little to eat if I threw it out, I decided to stuff and roast it. Henry was fine, Grace had an upset stomach, but I lay on the couch for two days and had to be treated for a bacterial infection back in the states.

Despite the challenges, I had a great time and was thrilled to have had a chance to go to Buenos Aires.

The next year, with anticipation in my voice, I said to Henry on the phone, "Where shall we go this Christmas?"

Henry said, "I thought we'd come to Raleigh."

"What?" (Long pause.) "You mean I have to buy a tree? Oh, no."

"Of course we're expecting a tree," he said.

Buying a tree, putting it on top of the car, cutting off the bottom of the trunk, and getting it upright in the stand seemed more than I could handle alone. They were arriving a day before Christmas, so I went to Walmart and bought a four-foot-high artificial tree that was covered with fake snow. When I tried to put lights on it, the green cords showed, so when Grace arrived, she wrapped all three strands of lights around the trunk. It was an interesting look.

After the holiday, when I had to take the tree apart to store it, I cursed this method. The strands of lights were intertwined. I tried separating the trunk into its three sections, but that made the problem worse. When I finally got the lights off and the tree parts stowed in the box, the floor was covered in fake snow. I vowed that I would not use lights next year. Instead, I ordered ornaments shaped like birds from the Internet in case I had to decorate a tree again.

In 2019, Henry said he wanted to come to Raleigh again for Christmas. I groaned. Almost all entertainment venues were shut down during Christmas week, so it was difficult to find exciting things to do. Henry didn't seem to mind. He said he rarely got a chance to just sit around and read. Grace likes North Carolina. I wanted to please my children, but this was not what I had in mind. I wanted excitement! I wanted to travel! I thought I had found travel partners in my children, but Henry and Keith had been all around the world—Asia, Africa, and Europe. Grace had gone to a wedding in Korea the past October. Sitting in a comfortable home with family was probably a nice change of pace for them.

Months later, we faced the COVID-19 pandemic quarantine. I was in the house by myself for months. We didn't expect a vaccine for a year or so. I looked ahead to Christmas 2020 and wondered what it would bring. I didn't think I would be able to see Grace and Henry. I fantasized about getting together with them during the summer in the Utah national parks (also on my bucket list). I would drive across country to meet them. It would take me about five days; it would be longer for Grace coming from Boston. I would sleep in my car at campgrounds on the way, and when we were together, we could each have our own tent and cook over a campfire.

When I said it out loud, it sounded like a tedious, long drive alone, but what was a lonely mother to do? Perhaps we would have a Zoom Christmas as the flu and COVID-19 roared through our communities. This year my gift would be the knowledge that we were all safe and healthy.

widow's brain

One afternoon, about a year after John died, I swept a metal detector back and forth in my wooded backyard searching for my husband's lost penknife. It was inlaid with turquoise and polished wood, and I had given it to him as a gift. He had lost it years ago and bought the metal detector then to search. If I had found it, I was sure the metal would be corroded and the wood eaten away by insects. My search unsuccessful, I returned to the house and had a good cry, although the tears didn't make me feel better.

A few nights later, I had a dream about John. I had driven to an ATM in the middle of a huge, empty parking lot. He drove by looking for me but couldn't find me. He drove slowly past me, stopped, and got out to look around, but never looked in my direction. I could see that he was calling me on his cell phone, but my phone was not ringing. I got out of my car and waved and shouted several times. Finally, he saw me. I woke up feeling good because we had connected.

It made me so happy to reconnect with John even if it was only in a dream. I wanted to reclaim what I had lost. Of course, it was futile. I had to chart a new course, one step in front of another.

I confided in a wise, older friend that I felt like I was a mess because I changed my mind every day. What sounded like a good idea one day seemed impractical or inappropriate another day. What was the matter with me? She said I sounded like a woman who had lost her husband and was finding her way. She was right; I had been desperately looking for a path forward.

In my search, I was constantly experimenting, assessing, and reassessing. I characterize most of the first year of my bereavement as a honeymoon period with myself. I was free to do whatever I wanted. I felt like a kid in a candy shop, trying new things, remaking my life. I made some bold moves, like remodeling my bathrooms. These turned out well despite my slow decision-making that dragged the process out over eight months. I bought two teak benches for the bathroom; I had yearned for something to set my robe on for years, but John had always vetoed furniture in the bathroom. I purchased three new sets of sheets for the bed. I refinished John's desk and chair and bought a new mesh desk chair for myself. I felt free to express myself and to buy anything I wanted, including clothing in boutiques, some of which I discarded a year or two later. Outdoors, I had twelve trees cut down and all the Elaeagnus bushes from the back yard removed. I bought a birdbath. John always vetoed this idea too, and said they bred mosquitoes. I took a clay class, and when I found my left hand was too arthritic to throw on the wheel, I rolled out clay slabs to make a Japanese-style lantern for the front garden. Slowly I was testing my limits and rebuilding a new life for myself, turning our home into my home.

Just as I acquired new things, I was discarding furniture and household goods I didn't need or didn't want any more. I churned the objects in my world as fast as my brain spun. Just as I think a new article of clothing will make me happier, I hoped these changes would do the same.

Eventually, my sadness rose in my conscious mind like the separation of oil and water. I realized what I had lost in John. I saw that the trappings of my life were not going to save me. I had been trying to sidestep my sorrow. It took attending bereavement groups, talking to other grieving people, and listening to their stories to start releasing my pain and beginning to heal. At home I started crying almost daily. I felt so fragile. So lonely.

I thought I'd like to spend summers in Boston to be closer to my daughter and old friends. I started brainstorming. Maybe Grace and I could share an apartment and split the rent. Maybe I'd buy a second house in the Boston area. We spent a weekend looking at houses, condos, and apartments, but practicality reigned. I had enough of a challenge managing one house, much less two. The memory of my hot water tank failing a day before I flew to Boston was fresh in my mind. And my daughter's good sense dampened any enthusiasm for living with her mother. I settled on renting a furnished apartment for myself the following summer. A practical choice.

Another grandiose fantasy I had was of buying a house in Raleigh and turning it into a homeless shelter for LGBTQ (lesbian, gay, bisexual, transgender, queer, and questioning) youth. Never mind that I had no skills in this area, I had passion. Over the years, I had met many kids who were kicked out of their homes because of their sexual orientation. This tugged at my heart. As I explored this possibility, I realized purchasing a property was only a very small step towards helping homeless youth. I would need a large, steady cash flow to maintain a house and fund staff that could work with this specialized population. Through my research, I found an organization in Charlotte that had a staff working with homeless LGBTQ youth providing them with case management, weekly meals, showers, groceries, housing services, and job training. I toured their impressive facility, talked to their executive director and housing case manager, and realized that donating to this organization was how I should channel my contribution dollars. In a sense, I came back to earth.

For most of my adult life, I have worn my hair all one length with bangs. About fifteen years ago, I tried a new hairdresser. She was from Trinidad, with long, curly hair and dressed in a colorful tiered full skirt, puffy blouse, and lots of bangles. She looked at my hair and said, "You have too much hair. It's too thick." She picked up her thinning shears and razor and gave me a pixie cut. It became my favorite cut, but no other stylist, including her, could ever recreate it. Moving south years later, my layered hair went every which way in response to the humidity, so I grew it back in. Longer hair was hot, but at least I could control it.

After John's death, I was feeling experimental, ready for another change, and had my locks cut in short layers again. My hairdresser was taken with the natural wave that appeared in the back, but the front bent into two giant flips on the sides, reminiscent of the Flying Nun or Bozo the Clown. My stylist tried to console me by saying that our hair changes as we get older. I kept thinking that I wanted my hair to lay like it did for most of my marriage. I want so many things to go back to the way they were when I was married to John. Whether my hair has changed or not, I haven't given up. I am still growing it out in hopes of taming the flip.

I don't want to believe that my mind and body have changed in the last forty years, but this is the double whammy of being widowed at this age. My husband is gone and I need to adjust to my aging body—things much more important than my unruly hair. Most of my years are behind me, not in front, so I need to curate my life carefully and use my time wisely.

When I think about my widow's brain, I think about all the new things I have tried or thought about doing. All the things that made sense at the time, but not later. It was like trying on clothes in the store. Is this me? How about this? Oooo, this is interesting, but where would I wear it?

I fantasized about changes I could make without anyone to answer to, about who I could be now that I had lost my former roles. It took trial and error, but eventually I became a new and improved practical self. However, I will never be finished with change because I like new perspectives. Periodically I rearrange the furniture in my house. It always feels like a fresh start.

scars

I wanted a new me. I wanted to be whole. I wanted to leave all my childhood and marriage bumps and scrapes behind. Part of that was a desire to be more attractive. Going shopping and buying new clothes makes me feel better. A new outfit is superficial, but it works. When I had my own business in the 1980s, I hired a wardrobe consultant and as a result bought a lot of new clothes. My new red silk dress made a big hit with business associates and personal friends alike. A woman approached me after a businesswomen's networking meeting and said "You are so successful." It felt good, but I thought, nothing has changed except my wardrobe. Obviously, appearances mattered.

I had warts removed from my face when I was a small child and as a result have scars on my nose, chin, and lip. Most people say they don't notice them. Occasionally a child points one out saying, "You have something on your nose." I cringe. Most of my life I have been unaware of them because I am looking out through my eyes at the world, not spending much time in front of a mirror. As an adult, I dabbed concealer on each of the four scars every morning to look my best. I even carried the concealer stick in my purse for touch-ups.

When my old college boyfriend, Phil, a cosmetic physician, visited a year after John died, I was nervous about my scars. He insisted on showing me his portfolio of patient before and after photos. I saw no difference as I looked at most of them. He was so enthusiastic that he detected a skin tag on my neck and wanted to slice it off on the spot. Getting to know him again made me feel more self-conscious about my face.

I made an appointment for an assessment with a local cosmetic dermatologist. I expected her to make suggestions and give me options that I could take home and mull over. She was ready to go to work right then. Although I just wanted my scars minimized, she saw so much more. She injected my cheeks with filler to plump them up, to reduce my slightly sagging jowls. She injected each one of my small scars to make them more convex instead of concave. She scraped bumps off my face. She took me into another room and zapped my spider veins with a laser beam. Each procedure was short, but painful. After I purchased their expensive face washes and moisturizers, they sent me home with an ice pack for my face. I couldn't sleep that night; my adrenalin was running from the minor assaults of the day.

Months later, after my face recovered from the mild bruising, the scars looked no better to my eye. The doctor suggested that we use micro-needling to abrade the scars and make them grow new tissue. She handed me off to an assistant who must have gone very deep on my chin because I ended up with two sizable, ulcerated wounds. The doctor was so concerned that she saw me on a Sunday and prescribed anti-viral, anti-fungal, and antibiotic drugs. I still have a deep indentation in the crease of my chin, but I pretend it is a dimple. I always admired Shirley Temple.

There were two more micro-needling sessions for my scars with another aesthetician who also needled my marionette lines. Some of us call those smile lines. I didn't see anything the matter with them. Although I was pleased with my minimized scars despite the thousands of dollars I spent over two years, I didn't see much difference between my before and after pictures. I was just happy that I didn't need to fuss around with concealer every morning.

We all have scars of some kind. Some people have positive associations with scars. They lead to stories of what a person has endured, whether it be bad acne or a childhood accident. They are badges of life, stamps of character. I look at my son and see the scar above his eyebrow when he fell from the high bar and we had to leave the playground much to his sister's chagrin. If I look very hard, I can see the faint scar from my daughter's cleft lip operation when she was a baby.

On the other end of the spectrum, scar tissue can reveal emotional damage or cause problems throughout our lives as we cope with a past trauma. What seems like a small slight to one person can leave lasting damage on a child. Certainly, surviving the loss of a loved one leaves an emotional scar. I didn't want my deep wounds from losing John to show. In the past, the tradition of wearing black signaled the trauma of loss so people would be respectful. Not all of us want to be so transparent. I refused to wear black to John's memorial services or afterward, partly because of my rebellious streak. At the time, I didn't see myself as wounded.

Looking younger did not factor into wanting my scars to disappear from my face. In years past, many people were surprised to find out I was older than I looked. I was so used to hearing this that in more recent years when young clerks in the grocery store tried to give me the senior discount, I was annoyed.

The scars on my face are superficial. My daughter Grace said I was ridiculous to try to have the scars reduced; no man would care about the scars on my face. Apparently, John didn't, but I don't want to take any chances for the future.

men

Is there a new man in your life? Are you dating anyone? Have you found a new partner?

I find those questions bewildering. Why are you asking me this? Are you assuming I have found someone new, and you want the details? Are you saying that I am so attractive that you would be surprised if I hadn't hooked up with someone after a year or two?

The first person who asked about my love life was someone I admire very much. I was surprised and hurt. I said, "No, I am still in love with my husband." She laughed. I didn't. I felt humiliated. Besides exposing my deep want, I felt like I was not measuring up, not doing what people expected of me. In other words, failing.

I couldn't imagine living without a partner, but that was not really what I wanted. I treasure time alone. It is like a quiet pool of water where lessons I have learned from John bubble to the surface. The space and time alone free me from the busyness of relationships, the how-was-your-days, the small conflicts, the old habits. I love change, the shake-up of old ideas. What's more, I was in no shape to pursue a serious relationship a year after he died.

I like having male friends, but since John died, I had not met many men with whom I wanted to pursue a romantic relationship. I felt ambivalent. On the one hand, I treasured memories of John, and on the other hand, I wanted to be released, to run away so I could pretend none of this had happened. Facing my loss and fears for the future was a tall order. I fantasized about having a new relationship because I didn't want to believe I would never have another partner.

Soon after John died, I created a list in my head of what I wanted in my next partner—someone a little more outgoing, more affectionate, more communicative. But I wondered how I could ever love someone who wasn't identical to John. As I pondered this more, my mind floated back to what John was like when I met him. I was attracted to his nice smile, but in his late twenties he was still finding himself and was a bit flakey. If I called him midweek asking if he wanted to go to a movie or a concert on Saturday, he'd say he needed to wait until that particular day to get in touch with his feelings. I don't think I would put up with that today.

The man who died was a completely different person from the man I knew in his twenties. The older John was confident, accomplished, and sure of himself. How did he change so much in thirty-six years? Did I change that much? In those early years, there was something that kept us interested in each other and committed to growing together. Maybe it was hormones.

I thoroughly enjoyed being married and benefitted great-ly from collaborating on projects and sharing our talents. I had lived with John longer than I had lived with my parents.

People who knew John towards the end of his life can't believe he was different when I met him. Besides being very intelligent and practical, he was reliable, responsible, and had a great sense of humor. The stability of being coupled had given him the opportunity to blossom.

So, if people change and grow, where should I begin if I want another relationship? Should I start with a diamond in the rough and hope for the best or, noting that I do not have another thirty-eight years to develop a relationship, should I look for a perfect match?

There were no perfect matches on the horizon, but soon after John died, I had some attention from Phil, who called every few weeks. We had once known each other very well and had always had some kind of psychic connection.

After college, Phil broke up with me mere weeks before I was to start graduate school in the same town where he attended medical school. I completed my degree in two years and planned to move to Boston. He knew nothing of my plans to move but stopped by the day before I left. His timing was amazingly coincidental.

Nine months after John died, Phil drove his truck down from New Jersey to North Carolina on a spring Friday for a one-day weekend with me. We had a nice but awkward time as we walked on eggshells navigating a relationship from forty years earlier. He was sillier than I had remembered. He'd tell jokes and make puns, then laugh hysterically. I cringed. At more serious times, he talked about the three women he was dating. How did he manage to date three women at once?

"I just check my text messages to review the previous conversations," he said.

At different times he would hold my hand and give me romantic signals. By Saturday afternoon, as we headed off to an upscale piano bar and dinner, I was emotionally spent and broke down crying in the truck. Through my sobs I said, "I am not going to be another one in your stable of girlfriends."

Nevertheless, as he headed north the next day, he sent me text messages filled with hearts and smiley faces blowing kisses. Ugh, I thought. Not my style.

Phil and I continued to be friends, and eventually the heart emojis dropped off. We had another visit or two. A year later, I stopped by Phil's house as I drove north to Boston with my cat Riley in 2018. On this trip Phil insisted on watching a television show called *Masters of Sex* based on the lives of sex researchers Masters and Johnson. I found it titillating and eventually became uncomfortable watching it. Phil had made it clear he didn't want to have a physical relationship with me, and I wondered why he continued to give me these confusing messages.

Sometime after my visit, Phil said that his most recent girlfriend had broken up with him because she didn't like the idea of me visiting. I didn't blame her. I met with Phil one more time the following October when I was near his home for my fiftieth high school reunion. We had lunch, and I heard about his latest girlfriend. This one sounded promising. I had always had the impression Phil was shopping for a wife since his second divorce. He said it was important to him to share his life with someone. That Christmas I texted him, he texted back, and that was the last time I heard from him. I was relieved. I have never been comfortable in the gray shades of life, and the ambiguity of our relationship stressed me out.

I pursued friendships with a number of men in the early years of my bereavement. I met Clark in a hot tub. We talked easily and were both interested in crafts and science. The day he told me he had a wood shop I was electrified. My father had had a woodshop, my husband had wood shop skills, so this was my idea of a real man.

I didn't have any plans for my birthday the second year after John's death, so I decided to invite Clark out to dinner. My treat. I wanted to go to a particular upscale area restaurant. He looked at the menu on the Internet and emailed me that he "ate vegan," and he could only eat a salad and a few desserts at that restaurant. My heart sank.

I trolled the Internet looking for a vegan restaurant and finally found one open on a Sunday night. It was not one of my favorite restaurants, but it would be okay. I called the upscale restaurant to cancel my reservation and told the hostess why. She said, "Oh, Chef loves our vegetarian and vegan guests. He will prepare something special for your friend."

Clark arrived at my house Sunday night and wanted me to drive to the restaurant. He said that highways made him nervous. As I drove us out of my village, he said, "I think I will have a steak tonight."

"What?" I said, "You said you were a vegan."

"Oh no, I'm not a vegan; I just eat vegan most of the time."

Uncomplimentary thoughts ran through my mind.

At the restaurant, Clark ordered a steak. The waiter looked puzzled because he had been told he'd be serving a vegan.

"Yes, I am as surprised as you are. Please apologize to the chef." I said to the waiter.

The evening was pleasant, and Clark and I continued to be friends. One day in the hot tub when I told him about a crafts gallery he might be interested in, he said, "Yeah, I'm interested if you'll drive me there."

I snapped back, "I'm not going to be your chauffeur."

Every relationship has its pluses and minuses, but this friendship was not heading in the right direction for me.

About a year after John died, I found a message on Facebook from another old boyfriend, this one from graduate school. Tim and I had met on our school's full-sized ice rink and spent every Saturday night for two years holding hands and gliding in circles. We had a wonderful relationship until he told me he was gay. I was devastated. I felt like I had let down all of womankind. That night I wandered the aisles of a supermarket like a zombie trying to find something to eat, but I had no appetite. He has since reassured me that I had not let down my gender, on the contrary. Before I saw his Facebook message, I had been searching for him on the Internet because I wanted to know that he had survived the AIDS crisis. I was delighted to find he was happily married and had retired from owning a printing plant. We emailed back and forth, and he had his own tales of loss to share. A year later, I visited him in New York City and had a great time reconnecting with him, visiting my old haunts, and seeing how the city had changed.

Back in North Carolina, I kept up a steady pace of activities to stave off loneliness and to make new friends. I enjoyed all kinds of dancing and drove to the next town several nights, bravely walking the few blocks alone in the dark from the parking lot to the hall. I tried to look casual as I waited for someone to ask me to dance. I didn't need too many partners because I became winded after a couple of dances. Then I'd sit down in a sweat and cool off for a few more dances before making myself available again. I enjoyed dancing with all the different people and body types, but some of the men were so fast at swinging their partners that I got dizzy.

One night I saw a man whom I recognized from a Quaker meeting. I tried to make small talk with him, but it was like pulling teeth. He told me he had a nonprofit company that gave away electric cars. I asked about his mission statement. He shrugged his shoulders. Hmmm. Later he told me his wife died of cancer, but he had made her work during the last two years of her life while undergoing treatment. Double hmmm. At the end of the night, he said something about getting together for coffee to talk sometime. I said, "Maybe." He put his contact information in my phone and wanted me to text him mine. I mulled this over for a few days then told him I was too busy to get together. That was no lie. I kept myself constantly busy. Mostly, I didn't want to struggle through a conversation with him.

One Saturday I headed to a food bank to attend an alumni event from my graduate school. I spotted a guy who looked about my age standing at a giant box of potatoes. I went over and stood next to the box. A woman with two pre-teens joined us. The woman was quite the conversationalist and peppered us both with questions, so we all got to know each other. She had been divorced for a year and a half; the man, Jack, had been separated for about seven months; and I had been widowed for a year. We all exchanged contact information. Jack followed up, but he made it clear that he didn't date. If I was interested in getting together as friends, he was game. So, we made a plan to meet at an outdoor café in my village and listen to bluegrass music.

While at the cafe, Jack ran into a friend from his divorce group. They both indicated that they were not dating so they didn't become "booty blind." This was a new term to me. Booty blind means getting sexually involved with someone soon after meeting them and ignoring signs that you may not be an appropriate match. Something to think about.

Jack and I went out to dinner and swing dancing once, but that was the last time I saw him. We didn't click. And, anyhow, he wasn't dating.

A couple of years later, I set a goal to join match.com. I wrote a profile and had my son give me pointers. I signed up for only six months to dip my toe into the water. After a month, I was tired of plowing through profiles, long and short, and writing messages to men who never answered or whose answers didn't impress me. The men who messaged me never hit the mark. Comments like "You have a nice smile" or "You seem like a nice person" weren't quite deep enough. What's more, match.com kept recycling the same profiles, many that did not match my preferences.

Three months in, I received a message from Tom, who looked interesting. He sent me links to sublime classical music, and he wrote in complete sentences with correct spelling and punctuation. We met for dinner, and he told me I was better looking in person than on match.com. I wasn't sure how to take that. My son said one of his dates had said the same thing to him. Maybe this was a family trait. Tom and I decided to meet again after Thanksgiving in a couple of weeks. I was going to Boston to be with Grace for the holiday. The next night, Tom called to chat. He told me many of the same stories he had told at dinner. He called the next night too, while I was packing for Boston and asked if I wanted to go target shooting with him sometime. He knew I had reservations about guns because he had made a point of telling me at dinner that he never hunted, only enjoyed the challenge of target shooting. Still, I was stunned. I told him I was a Quaker and anti-gun. However, always curious, I asked him what kind of guns he had. And how many?

I was not brought up in a gun culture, so I really don't know much about them. My only experience was tagging along when my uncle took my brother to a shooting range. I was about six. My uncle let me shoot the pistol once. That was enough. The gun's kick back was terrifying.

Tom said he used to have four pistols. He gave one to a friend who used to be in law enforcement, he had the one he used, he had an extra for someone like me, and there was the one he kept in his nightstand. I thought, well, you won't find me in your bed!

I didn't want to go out with Tom again. Guns were a non-starter for me. I went to Boston and talked to Grace about this. Every time I tried to role-play with her to refine what I wanted to say to end the relationship, Grace would emphatically say, "You're not in a relationship with him. You have no obligation. You don't need to make any excuses."

"But don't you think I should say…" I'd start.

"No. You don't owe him anything. You went out to dinner with him once."

"Wow, that seems harsh. Really?" I said.

"Really."

So, I sent him an email and simply said I wasn't interested in dating him.

Soon after this, I messaged someone on match.com who looked cute. He messaged back that he was a conservative. He said he needed to put that out front because it was difficult to find conservative women to date. His last two dates had ended badly. One woman slammed her hands on the table within two minutes of meeting him and stomped out of the restaurant. I was not exactly sure what he meant by conservative, so I asked for an explanation. He mentioned some conservative economic gurus. I was still suspicious. I had the feeling he told these women that he voted for Trump. Since we were being upfront, I asked if he had guns. He said no he didn't own any guns, but he took his grown son out skeet shooting every two years. We wished each other well and parted amicably. I was relieved when my match.com subscription ran out.

I decided that having friends vet possible dates might be a better strategy. I asked my friend Tad and his wife Mary if they knew any single men who were looking to date. Mary asked me about age range, interests, etc. She was very active in the Rotary Club and was thinking of three possibilities.

I said, "Well, I want someone smart with a good sense of humor and in his early seventies."

Tad looked hurt and said, "Wait. I'm 75."

"Hmm," Mary said. "Then Gerry is too old. He's eighty."

She and Tad bantered names back and forth, and then Mary said, "I know, let's have all three of them over for dinner and they can fight over Linda."

I grimaced. This was not going in the right direction.

Months later, when no phone calls were forthcoming, I had lunch with Tad and asked again about possible dates. He said there was a guy he played golf with who was really nice, but he walked slowly. I pointed out that I wore a brace on my knee so this was not a problem. When still no call came, I asked Tad again. He said that his friend was having back surgery. A delay. Then in early spring of 2020, we were all quarantined at home to avoid getting COVID-19. Now there was no hope of meeting anyone for a long time.

I wonder why people are attracted to each other. I don't think an Internet profile or a verbal description gets to the core of attraction. Having similar values doesn't guarantee a match either. When I hear friends complain about their spouses, I think that maybe I am better off alone. I cannot imagine what it would take to want to join forces with someone at this age. I suspect we were all more pliable in our younger years. In the past four years, I have relished running my own show, making my own decisions, living in my own calm.

a change of mood

Soon after John died, I would have told you that I wasn't angry about his passing. He had a good death—he didn't linger for years in pain, we had time to say what we needed to say, we planned his memorial services together, and he helped me prepare for a future alone. There was no blame, no reason to be angry. I was content to go places by myself. Being single was novel and felt liberating. I could come and go as I pleased. I could sit in a restaurant or on a bench and quietly observe and pay close attention. If I was with someone, I would have been concentrating on them, involved in our conversation.

Eventually the novelty wore off. I started losing my temper more easily. My daughter said she had never heard me swear very much before. Being alone became more difficult.

The second year after John's death, I was in the second phase of my bereavement. I had awakened from nine months of denial and spent the next nine months and beyond in the sad awareness of what I had lost. However, I still valiantly waged war against a slide into feeling sorry for myself and maintained my frenetic pace of activity. I was determined to live life to the fullest. I adopted the motto that if there was something I wanted to do, such as travel, I needed to do it now. After all, we never know when illness or accident will snatch life away. I was compelled to keep moving forward.

A seven-day cruise in the Western Caribbean with a group from my village sounded like the perfect travel opportunity. The idea of elegant accommodations and the sea air blowing through my hair was appealing. When I realized I would need to pay a single supplement to room alone, I recruited my bereavement buddy, Tad, to be my roommate. This was before he met his future wife, Mary. We had a chat over dinner before booking to alert each other to any strange personal habits. He mentioned his CPAP (continuous positive airway pressure) machine for sleep apnea but didn't say anything about his Waterpik. We were surprised to find that the bathroom didn't have electrical outlets, so he had to use the Waterpik in our room with the cabin wastebasket to drain the water. Yuck. Other than that, things went smoothly, and we were good roommates.

Tad and I signed up for some shore excursions together and went on others independently. He waded with stingrays while I toured Grand Cayman Island and went snorkeling. Together, we went kayaking in Key West and toured Xcaret in Mexico. Xcaret is an ecological theme park with an underground river, beaches, a Mayan village, two chapels, a Mexican graveyard, a hacienda, outdoor dining, an aviary, a butterfly pavilion, models of Mayan ruins, and dancing and music representing the various cultures of Mexico. It is one of my favorite places on earth. Eating lunch in an outdoor restaurant with a slight breeze and gazing across the palm trees at the beach below is my idea of heaven. John and I had visited Xcaret with Henry and Grace years before. I was grateful to be able to share this experience with a friend and not have to return to this paradise alone.

Our tour group of eighteen went in different directions during the day, but at dinnertime we ate at a cluster of linen-draped tables on the ship, sharing our daytime experiences. The group was made up of couples, one of which I knew, and two single women who traveled together regularly. The food was delicious, and the elegant dinners were punctuated by announcements from our extremely organized host couple. It was a congenial and jolly group.

After dinner the first night, we strolled out of the dining room, and I heard a band playing pop and R&B music. I was drawn to it like a magnet. The music pulsed through my body and made me move. I strutted out on the empty dance floor and started to pump my legs and move my hands and arms in time to the rhythms of the band. I was somewhat self-conscious that I did not have a partner, but not enough to keep me from dancing. Tad came out on the floor, but I knew he didn't feel comfortable dancing. The pain on his face prompted me to tell him to sit down, that it wasn't necessary to save me from impropriety. His was a kind gesture, but I valued my friend's comfort more than my desire for a partner. Eventually, another friend's husband joined me until lots of people danced with partners or in groups. Although the floor was empty every time I pranced out, couples soon appeared. I danced that night and every night of the cruise until I was too tired to rock any more.

One night a seven-year-old girl joined us on the dance floor. She danced alone too, and my friend Carole dubbed her the dancing queen after the ABBA song. I felt the title belonged to me. Dancing had given me agency. I was the one who encouraged the others to follow.

There is release in physical movement. Some find it through yoga, others through quiet walks or exhausting runs. I find it through dance. Music plays me like an instrument; I move because I can't sit still. I am wired to move when I hear music, whether listening to jazz or Mozart's *Requiem*. I feel happy when I dance. I beam. And, just as music makes me move, my voice teacher used to say I sang better when I moved my body. Music and movement go together for me.

Dancing on the cruise was a way to release my grief. Outside I was smiling, but inside I felt defiant. I had no partner, and I would show the world that I didn't need a partner, that I had every right to be on that dance floor whether I had a partner or not. I needed to be spun out like a top. I would have been happy to have the entire dance floor to myself—to spread my arms as wide as I wanted and to pound out my sorrow on the wooden floor. I try not to show my emotions, so this dance was in lieu of tears, an expression of the heartbreak of knowing I was now flying solo through life.

Most of the people on the cruise were coupled, including the large contingent of gay men from Canada. I chatted with couples I didn't know at breakfast, I watched couples stroll at our ports of call, I talked to couples in my group at dinner, I sat in single seats not taken by couples on tour buses.

Cruises seemed to be for twosomes, and I was surrounded by them.

When I returned home, I slipped into a funk. I realized that being on a cruise without my man took a tremendous psychic toll. I had expended so much energy being brave, insisting that I had a place on the dance floor and that I could travel by myself. It didn't help that I'd had a urinary tract infection for the duration of the trip. John had always wanted to go on a cruise, and I took him on one for his fortieth birthday. Now, here I was alone, twenty-nine years later, on my second and probably last cruise. I had signed up because I thought taking a trip with a group was an excellent opportunity.

A cruise was not the vacation for me. The couples orientation of the trip turned out to be a toxic environment, reminding me of my singleness and my loss.

What's more, I got seasick on all the tender boats that took us from ship to shore. I spent the entire forty-five-minute trip to a coral reef for snorkeling bracing myself inside of the bathroom, arms outstretched, palms on either wall, vomiting. I barely had the strength to snorkel when we arrived at the coral reef. I swam a short while, then left the group and paddled back to the boat where I lay down in a net hammock as the others glided below for hours searching for fish amid the choppy waves.

The melancholy of not having John with me contributed to my low spirits, but so did the realization that I was becoming more physically vulnerable. I started being plagued by motion sickness when I was twelve. I remember lying in the back seat of my parents' car as my father drove us through the Smoky Mountains. At age twenty-eight, I lay in the back of my friend's car while she drove us through the Alps. At age fifty, I gave up riding roller coasters. At age sixty-eight, being violently ill on a boat was a new low. The movement of the large ship didn't bother me, but the rides on smaller boats, where the rough waves challenged my control, made me physically ill.

The direct mail brochures from cruise lines used to look so enticing. After my experience, their advertising of half-priced river cruises annoyed me. I threw them out without even running my finger through the pages to break the wafer seals. The tempting prices were only for couples. Finding a travel partner was not an easy task.

It took practice to take the initiative to find a friend to see a movie or have dinner with me. As time went on, I got better at this, but when dates fell through and a friend cancelled a concert or movie date, I was disappointed and often stayed home. I didn't want to walk blocks alone at night from the parking lot to the venue. I found new ways to be social and at the same time useful. I started ushering at the local university repertory theater so I could see all the plays. I sat by myself in the theater, but I had a purpose and that felt good. I wanted to believe that I could handle widowhood, but at sixty-eight, being single again was a lot of work and not always fun.

medical challenges

I couldn't read street signs at night for more than ten years. I bought a GPS device to give me verbal directions, but that wasn't foolproof. I could still miss a turn. While John was alive, he drove when we went out at night, so my night blindness was rarely an issue. After he died, I used to have scary dreams of driving alone in the darkness where everything was a blur. I was feeling vulnerable. Now that I was on my own, I needed to resolve this issue. My doctor had been suggesting cataract surgery for a year, so I finally agreed. I needed to be able to drive safely if I wasn't going to be housebound at night.

Making the decision to have the surgery was easy compared to the other choices I had to make. Most people have their cataracts removed and new lenses put in to allow them to see distance without glasses. I was extremely near-sighted and always enjoyed being able to see fine detail by holding things very close to my eyes. My personality revolved around being detail-oriented. If I lost that ability, would it change my psyche? Carrying around reading glasses didn't appeal to me. What's more, I worked at the computer frequently and would need a second pair of glasses with a different focal length for the computer. I decided to have my eyes corrected for reading so I could retain some of my near-sightedness. I would wear progressive lenses for the computer and distance. I also thought I looked better in glasses.

Once I made those two decisions, I had to figure out how to manage all the additional doctor's appointments and self-care. I emailed friends to recruit drivers and offered to take them out to lunch if they would drive me to an appointment. This turned out to be very gratifying. I spent much more time with my friends than usual as we drove to and from the appointments, in addition to having lunch together. That gift of time with each of them turned out to be something I still treasure.

The second year after John's death, a stay in the hospital presented other challenges. For years, I had been plagued by urinary tract infections every six to eight weeks. My medical record showed multiple drug allergies to amoxicillin, cefuroxime, and cephalexin that limited the antibiotic palette doctors had to treat my infections.

While at my bereavement group one Tuesday night, I received a call from a doctor in my uro-gynecologist's service. I excused myself, took the call, and sat on a couch in the church lobby. The doctor told me I had an unusual infection, and they needed to treat me right away for five days in the hospital. The drug they wanted to give me could only be given intravenously.

Five days! I am an active person and could not imagine being tied down in the hospital for that long when I didn't feel sick. I had things to do at home. I needed to take care of my cats. I needed my computer. I imagined myself as a hospital captive wandering down to the nurses' station daily to straighten their desks or answer their phones. I needed to be useful and busy.

"Five days? Isn't there something else you can give me so I don't have to go to the hospital? Can I do an IV at home?" I asked, trying not to sound panicked.

The doctor was reasonable. And sympathetic. She discussed the pros and cons of my staying home, but eventually said that they needed to monitor me and that not being in the hospital could be dangerous.

I was swayed and called my cat sitter as soon as I got home. I immediately packed some comfy clothes and a canvas bag with magazines to last five days. The next morning, I drove to the hospital to check in. I was anxious but upbeat. I was relatively healthy and lucid. Fortunately, I wasn't going to the hospital badly hurt or unconscious with no one to advocate for me. I could handle this by myself. I was high functioning, a term doctors used to describe me, probably because I ask a lot of questions.

I sat amid large green plants in the admitting waiting area, listening to a volunteer play the piano behind me in the lobby. When it was my turn to see the hospital representative, I answered all her questions and gave Grace as my emergency contact. Later I found out that the staff member had assigned Grace the wrong last name and phone number. If anything had happened to me, the hospital never would have been able to reach her.

I was escorted to my room. It was clean and had a window, chair, television, and uncomfortably soft bed. I could choose three meals a day from a menu. Soon after I arrived, a young resident introduced himself, chatted for a while, and then copied all the drugs I took daily from the list I kept in my purse. He never asked about the order in which I took them, so the nurses doled out the pills every day in the order the pharmacy sent them. Each day I told the morning nurse that I was not supposed to take the blue pill until evening, so it didn't interfere with the large white pill I took in the morning. The nurses tried to take my preferences into account, but we were all getting exasperated going through this morning and night. I remained firm because this was my body; my regular doctors and I had worked out this schedule.

The pharmacist came to my room the second day. She questioned whether I was really allergic to amoxicillin since I had my last reaction when I was in my forties. She gave me a skin test for penicillin, an antibiotic in the same family as amoxicillin. It was negative. She convinced me to take amoxicillin while she waited for a half hour to see if I had a reaction. I did not. This was good news because the drug they needed to give me was related to these two.

I did not need to worry about being bored. There seemed to be a constant stream of doctors, nurses, and hospital staff in my room. In addition to the pharmacist and the resident, my own doctor visited with two other doctors after she was done with surgery. With each visit, I took notes to make sure I understood everything that I heard the doctors say. What was that drug they said they were giving me every twelve hours? What was the new drug they wanted to give me? By the end of the second day, they had all decided that I could go home with a PICC line (Peripherally Inserted Central Catheter) and administer the antibiotic myself. I was delighted.

The PICC line was inserted early on the third day. I was concerned that the insertion would hurt since I was awake and watching the procedure. It did not. The nurse was a pro. Once back in my room, I only had to wait for the home healthcare staff to write their orders and the nurses to discharge me from the hospital.

Camilla, a friend from my bereavement group, stopped in to visit before my discharge. We balanced a Scrabble board on the bed table and had fun playing despite the constant interruptions by nurses. I signed papers for my discharge and started to review the papers for my home healthcare when I realized that they had specified the wrong drug. I had taken notes; I knew what drug the doctors wanted. And I knew the doctors had changed their minds before settling on cefepime. I insisted the home health agency change it. They checked with the doctors and corrected the error. Then I signed the papers and left.

Yikes, I thought. First, they had my emergency contact wrong, then they were trying to give me the drugs in the wrong order, and now I was going to be given the wrong drug to administer at home. I felt very lucky to be able to be my own advocate.

As Camilla walked me out of the hospital, dragging my roller suitcase behind her, I felt very grateful that she had been there with me. She may have only been there a few hours, but it had a huge impact on my frame of mind. I did not know Camilla well, but the time she spent with me gave me the feeling that I was not alone in the world.

Going to a hospital solo is a dangerous proposition. Everyone needs an advocate, someone to ask questions, talk to doctors and nurses, take care of little things, take notes, and pay attention when the patient is too scared or nervous to think straight. This time, I didn't feel that I needed to call on friends to drive me to or from the hospital or stay with me. I was able to manage on my own, but I know there will be future times when more help is necessary.

At home, I was on my own again. Twice a day I scrubbed the IV connectors with alcohol before hooking up the medicine ball. As I did this, I remembered cleaning the IV connectors on John's port for one of his chemotherapy regimens. It amazed me that when I took care of this nursing chore for him, we assumed that he needed assistance. After all, we were a team. I wanted to help him, to be a part of caring for him, but now here I was doing this for myself. There was something sad about that. Sad that I had no one to clean my IV connectors, no one to help me. I wanted help. I had friends who cared about me, but I wanted someone so close that they would be here for me all the time.

I lay on my bed as the antibiotic drained into my arm and thought again about how much I appreciated Camilla staying with me until I was discharged and then walking me to the parking garage.

I suspect needing to rely on friends will increase as I age. I have always been an independent person, but being single at this age presents challenges. Whether I am gathering health-care information, trying to hang a picture by myself, or figuring out what to do with the rest of my life, I need my friends.

sinking

After two years of grieving, I was barely maintaining control of my feelings. I had worked so hard not to slip into depression. I stayed involved, developed my social network, remained optimistic, but had reached a point where I just felt tired—tired of being strong and tired of being responsible. I wanted to crawl in a hole.

I was desperately seeking a new purpose and filled my days with activities. I read to children at Head Start, worked with foster children, ushered at the local university theater, attended bereavement group meetings, took Spanish lessons, participated in aqua aerobics three times a week, joined two writing groups, sang with the village chorus, facilitated my spirituality group, lunched with friends, and took advantage of lectures and activities in my village. I don't smoke, drink, or use recreational drugs, so I self-medicated by maintaining a frenetic schedule. I didn't have time to think about John, my sorrow, my loneliness, or my future.

I tried to leave memories of John behind, to run from the pain of losing him, but he was still present. I had bathrooms remodeled, traveled to places we always wanted to go, went out with friends, and got to know men I never would have known while married. In many ways it was wonderful. All the time I would have put into my relationship with John, I spent doing things I wanted to do when I wanted to do them. There was no negotiating, no cajoling, no waiting until my partner agreed.

As much as I tried to forget John, reminders of him kept showing up in unexpected places. Charlie, from my bereavement group, slightly resembled John in physique, both of them rail thin and somewhat balding. Charlie's taste in clothing was similar to John's (and to my father's, for that matter). Several times Charlie showed up at our bereavement group wearing an identical fleece jacket or similar shirts to ones John had worn. One day I walked into the gym and there was my friend Chuck wearing the same Black Plague tee shirt I had reluctantly bought John for Christmas one year. He wanted it. I thought it was horrible.

I grew impatient. I wanted to move on. I didn't want to slog through messy emotions, let my guard down, or expose my raw underbelly. I just wanted to slide into a new relationship so I wouldn't be lonely. I would keep the pace going no matter how tired I was.

And I was very tired. I had been seeing a sleep psychologist who discharged me because she said I didn't have insomnia, which was her specialty. She passed me on to a sleep psychiatrist because I was waking up three to seven times a night. I was sleepy during the day, falling asleep in lectures, operas, bereavement group discussions, and while waiting at stoplights. In my first session with the psychiatrist, I described all the exciting things I was doing. She said, "I wish all my patients did that." I teared up a few times when I spoke of John, but that seemed reasonable since he had died a year and a half earlier.

"Do you want to know what I think?" the psychiatrist said after I finished. When I nodded, she said, "I think you are depressed."

"What? I just finished telling you all the exciting things I am doing. How can you say I am depressed?"

"You tear up every time you talk about your husband. When this behavior continues for more than a year, we say the patient is depressed. I'd like to prescribe a three-month course of Prozac. You can try it out. See how you feel."

At home, after I had time to process what she had said, I was incensed. How could she say that? I thought. I may be tired and anxious, but I am not depressed. I know what depression is, and I have no trouble getting out of bed every morning.

Grace happened to call that night, and I recounted what the doctor had said. Grace is a social worker and listened carefully. After a pause she said, "I can see that. Being depressed seems reasonable. Daddy hasn't been dead that long."

"What!" I was off again on my tirade, furious and feeling misunderstood.

The next day, I continued on my rampage at my women's spirituality group. I finished my story, head in hands, sobbing, "I want a boyfriend. No, I want a partner. No, I want my husband back."

A few members of the group gently suggested that I take the psychiatrist up on her offer to prescribe three-months' worth of the anti-depressant Prozac. Another member of the group later sent me a note with a list of therapists. I couldn't hide my distress from myself anymore. I wasn't just tired. I was confused and losing control. Whatever the psychiatrist wanted to call it, I definitely needed some guidance.

finding rest

John was comfortable with all things medical. I met him when he worked as the manager of the burn unit of a Boston hospital; later he managed a major hospital's operating room. During my twenty hours of labor before our son was born, John noticed that the Pitocin machine wasn't working and alerted the nurses. Years later when I had ankle surgery, he helped me interview surgeons.

John enjoyed being in medical research studies after he retired, and we both joined a study at Duke Eye Center before he became sick. While he had cancer, he participated in four studies at the University of North Carolina Cancer Hospital. It made sense that he wanted to donate his body to a medical school, but this turned out to be a challenging wish to fulfill.

While he was in hospice, I researched places that would accept his body once he died. Much to my surprise, he didn't meet the criteria for UNC Hospital's medical school where he was being treated. They wanted him to be above a certain weight (he was under 100 pounds when he died) and the build-up of fluid in his abdomen (ascites) was an issue. He was rejected by one or two other places before I secured him a spot at Duke University Hospital. Their Anatomical Gift Program accepted him after his hospice nurse spoke to them on the phone. I was so excited. I bounced into the bedroom and announced, "I got you into Duke!" It sounds morbid now, but I felt like I had gone through a rigorous college application process. "OK," he said. Understandably, his enthusiasm did not match mine.

When I was getting to know John, he told me that he wanted to be buried at sea because he had hoped to be a naval architect when he was younger. At the time, I thought that was weird. Now that I had been married to him for thirty-six years, I dreaded sprinkling his ashes in the ocean. It seemed so final, so inaccessible.

"What do you want me to do with your ashes?" I asked John one day while he was in hospice care.

"I thought we said we wanted our ashes spread on the hill we enjoyed so much in Vermont," he said. I did remember, but I recalled that I was the one who requested to have my ashes sprinkled there. I guess he had liked the idea.

When Duke Medical School students were finished dissecting John's body in anatomy class, the school had him cremated. It was a year and a half before I received the call to pick up his ashes. I retrieved the box from Duke and brought it home. I set it in the middle of the kitchen floor to see how the cats would react. Ebon walked away. Riley, who had been devoted to John, gave the box a thorough sniffing. I sat there for a while pondering the ashes. Crying, I thought, I am not

157

letting you go again. I can't give you up to the earth. I'm going to buy a beautiful urn and display you. A few weeks later I went to an upscale gallery and bought a large hand-thrown vessel swirled with John's favorite earth-tone colors and put most of the ashes inside. The rest of the ashes I spooned into three zip-lock sandwich bags for a trip to Vermont.

Henry and Grace had agreed to travel to Vermont with me for an informal ceremony in June 2018. I would be spending the summer in Boston, Grace lived there, and Henry would be in Boston on business.

In June, the three of us drove to Vermont and had a lovely weekend. It was beautiful weather, and I was grateful to spend time with my children. On Saturday, we hiked into the woods where we sprinkled our bags of ashes on the slope John and I had chosen. A slight breeze caught John's remains as Henry shook the last of the gray dust from his bag. Grace snapped the image with her camera. I will hold the loveliness of the scene in my memory forever. We lingered and then hiked back towards the inn where we were staying. Grace and Henry took the long way, but I was tired and walked directly back.

I had had no crying jags during our informal ceremony, only a tightness in my chest, a feeling I had experienced a couple of times since John's death. Is this what it means to have a broken heart? I mulled over my doctor's warning to go to an emergency department if my previous chest tightness recurred. Going to the hospital seemed like an inconvenient way to interrupt an idyllic weekend. I walked slowly back to the inn, took a nitroglycerin pill, and lay down. This, too, would pass.

something old, something new

For my second Thanksgiving without John, I flew to Boston to see Grace and have dinner with a large group at my Quaker meeting. The caretaker of the meeting house used to be a caterer, and it was always a treat to be at one of her events. I also went to Boston to explore real estate because I wanted to spend summers in Boston. Eventually I found a furnished, short-term rental apartment and put a deposit on it for the following summer.

I missed Boston, but I loved living in North Carolina because I had made more friends there in one year than I had in twenty-five years in the Boston area. However, the friends I made in my Boston Quaker meeting were deep friendships that had been built over decades. In North Carolina, I yearned for the deep comfort of that community. And I wanted to escape the hot, humid summers in the piedmont of North Carolina. I sweat so easily that when we first moved south, I sometimes took three showers a day.

Before flying back to North Carolina after Thanksgiving, I stopped in Pennsylvania to visit a favorite spot from my childhood, Longwood Gardens. I remembered it as magical during the holidays because they decorated the buildings and wrapped the tree branches with lights. Seeing it as an adult, fifty years later, it was less impressive, but I still enjoyed the visit.

While in the area, I stayed with my old boyfriend Phil. We went driving in the country in his son's sports car, and I asked him to take me to Millersville, a small town where my surrogate grandparents had lived. My mother had lived with this couple when she taught in the area for two years to get her teaching license. I remember their bungalow-style home vividly, the living room spanning the front, the wide stairs to the second floor, the big kitchen, and the water pump on the enclosed back porch. Being allowed to lift the pump handle up and down to see the water pour out was always the highlight of the trip for a school-aged me.

Millersville is not very big, so I was sure I could find the shady, tree-lined street they lived on. I couldn't find anything that remotely resembled it. The terrain held no memories, and I began to feel as if I had made up this recollection. I kept thinking, it's true, you can't go back. Things change.

I spent the rest of my second year of bereavement planning my summer adventure in Boston. How would I get two car-sick cats there? What would I need to take? Who did I want to notify that I was coming? Who could I visit on my drive north, and where would I stay? There was nothing like planning a project to make me feel alive and give me purpose.

In June, Grace flew to North Carolina to pick up Ebon, my cat who was more prone to nausea than the other, even when medicated. I met her at the airport and handed off Ebon and his suitcase. It is amazing how much luggage a cat can have—scratching box, litter box for the airport, small bag of litter, dry food, wet food, water, medication, towels, toys, halter, and leash. They flew back to Boston together that same day. The next morning, my other cat, Riley, was medicated for car sickness, and we started driving north.

I took my time driving since I tended to fall asleep at the wheel. However, the trip proved too eventful to get drowsy. After I had stopped for lunch one day and was waiting to pull on to the highway, I felt a jolt, heard a thud, and knew I was rear-ended by the young man in the car behind me. He was very polite but upset because he was on his way to meet his parents. As unfortunate as this was for both of us, I watched as he took out his phone and snapped a picture of my license and license plate. Perhaps he'd had this type of experience before. I had never thought of using my phone camera but followed suit and took pictures of his documents and the damage. The day was not a total loss since I had learned something new.

I met my college friend Gale and her husband Jim at a restaurant for dinner that evening after sequestering Riley in the motel room. I hadn't seen my friends for years since Jim's work took them all over the world. I liked renewing my connections, except when the talk turned to my new widow status. I was constantly chagrined that I did not have John by my side.

Driving alone had its challenges. I could have used John to navigate. Even though I had a navigation system in my car, it seemed to get confused in the busy Washington, DC, area. I thought I had requested one particular route, but it started to take me on another. Trying to figure out where I was while driving and to change course was very frustrating. Another time, I was desperately looking for a bathroom and got off an exit, but all I could find was a flea market. That turned out fine because I decided to buy lunch there too.

Fortunately, Riley was a good sport and eventually got used to traveling. The first couple of days he cried the first half hour in the car, but eventually settled down and slept most of the time. As I got more comfortable with him riding next to me, I unzipped the top of his carrier so he could look out every now and then. Most nights I stayed in motels instead of with friends because I had Riley with me. No matter where I stayed, I made multiple trips lugging his paraphernalia into the room each night. I had one personal item; he had several.

In Boston, the cats and I settled into our rented apartment. Grace had stayed there with Ebon after flying back to Boston and had stocked the kitchen. I was grateful. Driving three and a half days with only a cat as navigator was stressful. It took me a week or two to recover.

As the summer passed, I was surprised how much time I spent with Grace. She was working full time, but occasionally would bring food from her prepped-meal service and cook it at my place. Her boyfriend was often unavailable at dinnertime since he worked in a restaurant. She would hang out with me for the evening, usually perusing her phone. Hanging out is a skill I have never developed. I have always been a business-like, no-nonsense person. My parents used to say with aggravation, "Relax!" Obviously, this never worked, but Grace was able to demonstrate the technique quite well. I learned to emulate her and check my email on my laptop in the living room while she lounged on the couch. Occasionally, we went out for dinner or took a day trip. She is easy to be around, and it was wonderful to have so much time with her.

I was delighted that my son Henry was in Boston on business for part of the summer. This was very exciting because I usually only saw him once a year at Christmas. He invited me to a lunch meeting to hear him speak about the design system he had developed for the air force. Seeing my son present so expertly was a thrill.

Henry, Grace, and I managed to go to dinner and a movie one night and, later in the month, to Vermont for the weekend when we sprinkled John's ashes on a mountain slope. At dinner that night, I sat quietly. Grace and Henry chatted away, but I seemed to have nothing to say. I was more observer than participant in the conversation. Was I in a reverie or were they talking about things relevant to young people, not a retired, somewhat recent widow?

One Sunday afternoon, the three of us and Grace's boyfriend Charles had dim sum in Chinatown. Another time, we had dinner at an Afghan restaurant. The three of them chatted about beer and breweries. As a non-drinker, I had nothing to add to the conversation and again felt a bit irrelevant. The obvious age difference was beginning to feel disconcerting.

Grace and I took one more trip that summer. At the end of June, we flew back to the heat and humidity of North Carolina to attend a memorial service in Duke Chapel for the families of anatomical gift donors. I had no idea what to expect but was pleased to hear students speak about their experiences with their cadavers. One student put it this way:

"Your loved one has been my very first patient, my best teacher, my mentor at times, my companion as I learned the complexities and beauty of the human body. As I recall the orientation of any organ or texture and strength of a specific muscle, your loved one is the first to come to mind before any textbook image or professor's descriptions."

Grace was struck by the number of donor families with young children that were present. She told me she felt thankful that she'd had her dad throughout her childhood, and it moved her to realize these children would miss that.

Each family was presented with a basket of flowers and a booklet of handwritten letters from the students expressing their gratitude. We walked from the chapel to Duke Gardens, where a lovely indoor reception was held. It was a hot day, so we were happy to stand in the food line while being cooled by air conditioning. Afterwards, we braved the heat and humidity to walk around the gardens until we wilted. It was a lovely, gratifying afternoon.

In July, I started volunteering with a group of homeless artists hosted by Common Arts, a ministry of Boston's Common Cathedral. The organization provides space, art materials, and support staff to the homeless population of Boston each Wednesday. In addition to painting, sculpture, and fabric crafts, Common Arts had a large group that created beaded jewelry. I spent most of my hours there sorting discarded beads into bins so they would be organized for the next artist. Sometimes I staffed the sewing machine and repaired backpacks and clothing, a rewarding task knowing that some of these folks lived out of their backpacks. One day when the machine stopped working, I was amazed that one of the homeless artists was able to fix it. His mother used to have a sewing business, and she had taught him how to repair the machines.

There was a lot of talent among these artists. One woman knitted beautifully, and she told me she also played the piano. As we chatted, her words revealed she had very low self-esteem and became easily frustrated with her projects. I wondered what could have happened to derail a person with so much talent. Did she have a mental illness, a deficient upbringing, lose her job, and subsequently her apartment? It made me ponder the fragility of each of our existences. There but by the grace of God go I. I needed to be careful not to make a false move as I wandered through the no man's land of widowhood.

Years ago, John and I took our children to a women's soup kitchen to expose them to some of the ways other people lived. After serving dinner, we sat down with a homeless woman to eat our meals. After chatting with her and noticing the large diamond ring she wore, I realized that at one time she had had a higher standard of living than we did. That experience reminded me that we are never guaranteed to always have the privileges we enjoy today.

Each week at Common Arts, the artists who wanted to sell their work hung their wares on wire mesh racks for other artists and the public to view. One piece caught my eye. It was a dragon painted in a wash of blues and greens that had wild eyes and a discombobulated look on its face, as if he was scared. It drew me in. It spoke to my emotional side. I kept coming back to it. What I saw in the dragon's face expressed how I felt about my future. I hadn't been aware of my fear. I took the picture off the rack and paid the asking price of $30. I carefully carried it home on the train and displayed it on my bureau in my apartment. This art revealed feelings I could not, nor dare to, share.

At lunchtime on Wednesdays, I walked the couple of blocks to the Boston Public Garden. It is a wonderfully landscaped area in the middle of downtown Boston with a pond, huge shade trees, and a series of formal plantings. Each season the flower beds are dug up and replanted with a different array of annuals. In the many years I lived in Boston, I was always too busy to sit in the Public Garden and enjoy it. I often parked next to the garden for an appointment and, afterwards, sped off before my parking meter ran out. But now, as a tourist, I had time to appreciate it.

As a woman alone, I was watchful, but not afraid of being accosted by someone who looked strange to me. We are probably all strange looking to someone. There were teenagers in cut-off shorts and shirts that barely covered their chests, a guy selling water on the corner who couldn't speak but liked to joke in pantomime, women in stiletto heels and flowing hair walking at a clip, men and women weathered and worn from living on the street, police mounted high on their horses, button-downed business people, mothers with strollers talking on cell phones, dog walkers, and individuals like me sitting alone on a bench eating lunch. Resting in the cool shade amid manicured gardens and the meandering walkways refreshed me each lunchtime. I loved being in this city.

The experience of working with homeless artists made a huge impression on me. I didn't always feel useful, but I learned things from people whose paths I would not have crossed without volunteering with this community. I came away from the summer reminded that there is "that of god in every person." I may have lost my husband and life as I knew it, but I had a home and a support system; I was not mentally ill and not in the unfathomable position of making untenable choices such as living on the street.

The rest of the summer was comfortably busy. I visited museums with old friends or alone—the Museum of Science, the Isabella Stewart Gardner Museum, the Peabody Essex Museum, the Concord Museum, a quilt museum, and a small telephone museum. I joined a Meetup group that went to the movies and dinner every Sunday afternoon. I went to a jazz service in one church and took a self-guided tour of Tiffany stained-glass windows in another. I joined the YMCA for aqua aerobics and went on a canoe outing with a friend. Remembering my past, I visited a revered older friend in hospice and, looking towards my future, I toured a continuing care retirement community. And of course, I went to my Quaker meeting on Sundays, our independent worship group every other Saturday, a program at the meeting house each Wednesday night, and my small spiritual growth group once a month.

I wandered the streets of downtown Boston marveling at the changes since my last trip. There were parts I used to know well that I didn't recognize. The Rose Kennedy Greenway snaked through the business district—new parks and gardens, a merry-go-round, and a fountain for children. It was wonderful to be a tourist in this city where I had lived for close to forty years.

Returning to Boston for the summer was a way to connect with my past. I wasn't looking for John there, but myself. I wanted to see what I had once loved. I had rich conversations with old friends and heard about their current lives—their children, their husbands, their musical careers, their illnesses, their vacations. I even had lunch with my old boss from the Museum of Science. We ate in a nearby elegant restaurant, which was a jail when I lived in Boston.

In July, I took the train to New York City to visit my friend Tim from graduate school. We saw a show in Harlem's Apollo Theater and a revival of *Carousel* on Broadway. Despite his Parkinson's disease, Tim could walk for hours. And we did. We walked from his co-op on West 123rd Street, across Central Park, and down to the Metropolitan Museum of Art on Fifth Avenue at East Eighty-second Street. We walked on the High Line that opened in 2009 down to the site of Tim's first print shop. We walked through Greenwich Village to the East Village where I used to live. My old address on East Tenth Street looked a lot nicer and safer than when I had lived there. Things had changed in the last decades.

By the end of July, Henry had flown back to California, but Grace was available to have dinner with me on the anniversary of John's death. I chose a restaurant on the waterfront that John and I had enjoyed sixteen years ago. We had waited there to drive Henry and his date back home after a prom night cruise. I love eating outside, particularly on the water with a gentle breeze blowing. The romance was gone, but Grace and I had a lovely evening as we strolled along the waterfront park after dinner. At one point Grace asked if I thought about John very much. I said, "I try not to, it makes me too sad."

My time in Boston ended in late August, but I had one more trip planned for October, my fiftieth high school reunion. Each trip to the past reminded me that time and I had moved on. People's lives change. My life had changed. The summer I spent in Boston was like taking a vacation, but I was glad to be home in North Carolina and felt renewed.

turbulence

After summering in Boston, I felt centered and more confident. I had grown and, in the process, I had shed old habits. My gardens at home had flourished and produced a healthy crop of weeds, and the yard was covered with three-months of tree droppings. My wonderful next-door neighbor had dragged his hose to my yard and watered the rhododendrons and Lenten roses that we had transplanted from his yard in the spring. The lantana I planted in John's memory was the biggest surprise. Barely six inches high when planted, it was now a bushy three feet tall. John had always admired the pretty yellow, orange, and pink flowers on our neighbors' lantanas along the street, so this was the perfect memorial plant.

John used to do most of the outdoor work. I enjoyed doing yard work too, but I tired much faster than he did. When we were younger and raked piles and piles of leaves off our Massachusetts lawn, he always knew when I had overextended myself. "Linda, you're tired. Go in the house." I think it was my crankiness that tipped him off.

When we purchased our house in North Carolina, we chose a wooded lot, assuming yard work would be minimal since there was no grass. We quickly learned that there was plenty to do. Sticks seemed to fall out of the trees at a faster rate than they did in Massachusetts. Although I love pine trees, every year brought a crop of pinecones. I discovered that our yard was filled with pinecone landmines as each year's harvest was covered with a blanket of pine needles. The woodsy floor looked lovely, but my weak ankles struggled to walk around the yard.

I emailed my landscaper to have him clean up my yard. Good landscapers were difficult to find. I had hired the same man for years and was pleased with his work even though he rarely got back to me as quickly as I wanted. Weeks went by without a response, so I texted him. More time elapsed without a word. I was expecting guests in the next couple of weeks and wanted the yard to look good. I had a free afternoon, so I had time to do this. I decided to do the work myself.

I put on long pants, a long sleeve shirt, an old pair of shoes, and sprayed myself with bug repellant. I ventured out and picked up sticks, pulled tall weeds with fringy tops, and used the sole of my shoe to rub off the small weeds that grew between the bricks on the front walk. I made the yard look presentable. After hours of work, I corralled the yard waste into a barrel and a pile in the back yard, ready to drag deep into the woods.

I don't know if it was a pinecone, root, or stone that I stepped on as I turned, but I fell and twisted my left knee as I went down. This was the same knee I injured four years earlier when recovering from ankle surgery. The complex tear in my knee's meniscus was once again inflamed. As I lay there,

I said to myself, "That's it. I'm done. I can't do this anymore. I'm moving." I was done trying to tame the woods alone. Done trying to care for an acre and a third alone. And, done trying to cajole my landscaper to call me back. I also needed to be done with fastidiously picking up the yard the way I picked up my house.

When Henry and Grace had visited the spring before John's death, I asked them to help me work in the back yard. Grace and I picked up sticks and put them in piles that Henry hauled back into the woods. When we were almost finished, Henry said, "Why are we picking up sticks and moving them to a different part of the woods?" It struck me then that someone as detailed as I am would go crazy trying to keep the woods pristine.

I picked myself up off the ground and limped into the deep woods, dragging the yard waste. Back in the house, I cleaned up, iced my knee, and kept it elevated. I sat there and fretted because we were expecting Hurricane Florence and I needed to go out and get supplies. I could ill afford an injury.

I dreaded this hurricane because I had never been through a major storm without my father or my husband. John knew what to do in emergencies, how to prepare, and how to hunker down. I would meet the challenge myself, but I felt vulnerable. Weathering a storm alone was bad enough, but now having trouble walking compounded my anxiety. It made me feel even more defenseless.

I sat on the couch with my ice pack and leg elevated making a mental list of what I could buy to eat if the power went out. I had an electric stove. Should I try to fire up the outdoor grill? I would need to buy propane and hook it up. This terrified me. John had bought the grill. I didn't know how to use it and never wanted to know. I settled on a plan to use some large aluminum pans with a wood fire if it became necessary. On the other hand, cold beans were fine with me.

I hobbled to the car with my shopping list. At the store, I threw away my pride and sat down on one of the electric carts for disabled people. After all, I needed help to get around the store. I was familiar with these carts from having used one when I had my ankle surgery. At that time, John had been there to show me how to unplug it, turn it on, and steer. That tutorial came in handy now. I purchased my groceries and made it home before the rain began. There was wind and rain for days, and occasional power outages, but no damage to my house. I actually enjoyed hunkering down with my cats. We did fine.

The day after the rain stopped, I took Riley to the cat hospital for a three-day visit. He had been diagnosed with hyperthyroidism in Boston and now was getting a radioactive iodine treatment to kill the errant thyroid cells. On the third day, I waded through water to pick him up, then took Ebon to our regular vet because he was acting ill and hadn't moved his bowels for days. The vet gave him subcutaneous fluids, stool softeners, and an enema, none of which worked.

Two days later the vet had to dig out his bowel under anesthesia. We went home with prescriptions so I could prepare his food every morning and evening with two liquid medicines to keep his colon working, powdered fiber, a powdered supplement for his joints, an analgesic for his arthritis, and his Prozac (to keep him from harassing Riley). He was woozy for two days, wandering in circles with dilated eyes, only to land in his litter box where he stayed for hours each time.

We had a relatively calm week before I spent the weekend doing chores. On Sunday, I went to the dump and drove quickly through the stations for trash and recyclables. At the last one, I stopped to drop off glass jars. When I jumped out of my car, I must have forgotten to put it in park. As I stepped out with a plastic bag of glass to recycle, the car started to move forward and threw me off balance. I fell on my hands and knees, crushing the glass in the bag with my left hand. I stood up and watched my car roll across the blacktop, through the gate, across the street, and into the woods. As blood dripped from my hand, I thought, hmm, how do you handle a situation like this? Should I tend to the car or my hand first? Always concerned about neatness, I bent down, picked up the broken glass, and threw it in the trash.

A man parked in front of the woods shouted, "Do you need help?" For the first time in my life, I didn't pretend to be unfazed and brush him away with, "No, no, I'm fine." Instead, I looked at the blood pouring from my hand and said, "Yes, I'm hurt."

He got me some clean rags, and then the staff at the dump ushered me into their shed where they ran water over my hand and tried to stop the bleeding with paper towels. They called an ambulance (that cost me $859) to take me to the emergency room and notified the state police so they could get my car out of the woods.

For me to admit that I was hurt or couldn't handle a situation was a milestone. I always liked to feel that I was in control. Now I was in a situation that I wasn't sure how to handle. What do you do when you can't call your husband and say, "I've had an accident. Please pick me up."?

I spent the first year of my widowhood acting like nothing had happened to my interior self. My husband had died, but I was convinced I remained the same. Even if I hadn't changed during that time, I had to change now.

The ambulance ride was a revelation. I pictured being carried in a gurney and attended to by EMTs. Instead, I had to hoist myself into the back of the truck and sit on a hard seat as the EMT took down my personal and insurance information. The gurney in the middle of the vehicle was loaded with equipment. It was clear I wouldn't be lying down. When the ambulance started up, I looked for something to hold on to with my good hand, but there were no straps to grab or to tether me in. I was on my own as we whizzed down the highway. I lurched forward as we stopped at every traffic light.

When we arrived at the hospital, the EMT checked me in and waited until a staff member took me off his hands. She cleaned up the bleeding hand and wrapped it in some gauze that was quickly saturated by the never-ending flow of blood. I sat in the waiting room for three hours wondering when I would be seen. The man next to me indicated that I was dripping blood on the gym bag that had been retrieved from my wrecked car along with my purse. I went to the ladies' room and tried to wash the blood off my arm and bag, and to add a layer of paper towels to soak up more blood.

I called my friend and neighbor Peg and asked her to feed my cats. She walked across the street to my house and called me. I described Ebon's various medicine bottles and how much medicine to mix in his food. She said she would come and sit with me in the hospital and asked if I wanted something to eat. I asked her to bring the leftover appetizers that I had served her and her husband the evening before at a small dinner party. She arrived an hour or two later and gamely sat next to a basin of bloody water and listened to me scream as a resident and medical student injected my left hand with anesthetic and closed my wounds with fifteen stitches. Peg drove me home around ten-thirty p.m. and kindly offered to spend the night. As she drove onto our street, we saw that our neighborhood was pitch black. The power was out. Somehow, we made it into my house. I asked her to unscrew the child-proof tops to my medicine before she walked across the street to fetch some lanterns for us to use.

The next day, Peg drove me to the pharmacy to pick up an antibiotic and to get a tetanus shot that the emergency department doctor said I needed. Unfortunately, the hospital staff had neglected to give me the tetanus shot in the hospital or hand me a prescription for the antibiotic. After numerous phone calls to the emergency department, the hospital's orthopedic urgent care, my own doctor's office, and a very kind local pharmacist, I was able to get the antibiotic and injection. Peg even drove me to the tow yard holding my car. We walked around the car, stooping to survey the damage done to the undercarriage as my car rolled through the brush and came to rest against a tree. We couldn't see much, so we opened the hatch and rescued a few things I thought were valuable.

What would I have done without Peg? Who would have fed my cats? Where would I have gotten food while waiting in the emergency department for seven hours? Would I have taken a taxi home at ten-thirty at night to a dark house? Peg filled in for John by being my best friend. I will always be grateful for her sensitivity in foreseeing my needs at that critical time.

My hand was sore for a few days. Eventually I rented a car and had my damaged car moved to a repair shop. The estimator suggested I go car shopping over the weekend. I headed for Subaru, test drove a new Forester and Outback and a few days later bought a 2019 Outback. It was a newer version of my damaged car and in the same color.

Despite the stress, I kept up my usual pace—weeks filled with meetings, lunch dates with friends, and volunteer gigs. As I look back at my packed calendar, I wonder how I managed. Shouldn't I have holed up in my house for weeks to rest and repair? I had survived a fall in the yard, a hurricane, two sick cats, a badly cut hand, seven hours in the emergency department, and the purchase of a new car. Didn't I need time to slow down, reflect, and absorb all the stimulation?

Maybe so, but that's not what I do. I had headaches for weeks and was somewhat depressed, but I kept going. And, ever the optimist, I was expecting some fantastic luck soon.

the house

Within months of John's death, I requested bids from contractors to remodel our three bathrooms. I relished the thought that I could make all the decisions myself. There was no one to question my color or tile choices. In our first house in Massachusetts, it took two years to convince John to go with dark blue flowered wallpaper to set off our white tiled bathroom walls. He loved it when it was done. This time, I chose new faucets and granite counter tops, but cautiously waited another six months before having the shower and floors retiled. I was pleased with the result.

A year after the bathrooms were done, I was still feeling restless. I often joke with friends who are thinking of remodeling, that it probably means they actually want to move. It was true in my case. I was looking for change. Just as I didn't remodel the bathrooms in one pass, the realization that I wanted to move came slowly. Once the idea was planted, I argued with myself daily. Every time I looked out the window at the woods that surrounded my house, I said to myself, "You'd be crazy to leave all this." I loved the setting of our house.

Indeed, I was crazy. Crazy to get out of my skin. Crazy to live another life. Crazy to run away from the grief, the fear, and the sadness.

Part of me felt guilty wanting to move from the home John and I had created together. He was part of the house. But I knew I had to make this transition, so I reassured John that he was coming with me. After all, our memories were in my heart and mind and would be with me always.

There were practical reasons for moving. I wanted a smaller, cozier home so I would feel safer. I lived in the woods and knew if I screamed no one would ever hear me. My house had a long floor plan with a bedroom wing at one end and a country kitchen at the other. If I left my phone in the bedroom, I couldn't hear it ring if I was in the kitchen. In the morning the house felt empty as I walked down the hall on my way to breakfast, past a silent living room and a pristine dining room. I spent most of the time in the big country kitchen where a couch awaited in front of the television. When John and I moved into this house, we thought the cooking area was much bigger than we needed. The refrigerator was closer to the couch than the sink. We remodeled the kitchen to move the fridge a foot or two closer to the workspace, but it still seemed to be too many steps away. Most people like big kitchens, but not me.

Taking care of the one and a third wooded acres was a challenge for me. Neighbors and friends found landscapers just as unreliable as I had. Many yard care companies had reputations for having rigid fertilizer and weed control protocols. To protect the cats, John didn't want Roundup used in the yard, so I continued to insist on this. I needed a low-maintenance home with a small yard.

I thought I wanted to live in the village, a neat cluster of homes surrounding a big, landscaped park. I would be near more people and feel less isolated. I loved living surrounded by trees, set far back from the road, but the large frontage came with a long driveway. When it snowed, I had to shovel it by myself.

While the gears in my mind were turning, friends from my bereavement group were making their own decisions. Some forged their own plans, some had adult children swoop in and take over, and some had the good fortune to meet new partners. A few stayed in their big houses. Many moved to apartments, condos, or retirement facilities, and some bought new houses with their new wives or husbands. All of our paths were different.

My friend Betty from my bereavement group had outlived two husbands and a partner. When the conversation in our informal dinner group turned to the question of whether we should sell or keep our homes, Betty put her hand on my arm and said, "You don't need to worry about this. When it is time to sell your house, you will know." Betty was right.

I was well prepared to buy a house on my own. We had owned three different houses in over thirty years. When there were major remodeling projects or additions to be built, I was the one who worked with the architect and builders. I was a natural organizer, a detail person. And I had sawdust from my dad's workshop in my veins.

Puttering around the house, fixing things, building, and creating were the most enjoyable parts of my marriage. John and I worked well together. Sometimes I started a project and John took over when I asked him for help. Sometimes I was his helper, handing him tools or running to find a needed part in one of our toolboxes—a slotted wood screw instead of a machine screw or a rubber mallet instead of a claw hammer. I learned a lot from John. My father's woodshop had sparked my interest, but John took the time to show me how to cut a dado joint or how to use a socket wrench. Most of this came by osmosis—watching him or accompanying him to the hardware store as he bought tools or supplies.

Many of the memories I would leave behind by moving were projects that John and I had planned or completed ourselves. Our kitchen was our first big project. We designed it with a similar flow to our kitchen in Massachusetts, but had pros build and install the cabinetry. We painted walls, including the bright blue accent wall behind the counter. John always wanted happy colors. That one certainly was. We hired a professional landscape designer to plant our front slope. We had laid the brick patio and walkway in our Massachusetts house, but we hired someone to do brickwork for us in North Carolina. Then John needed to create an elaborate drainage system to keep the walkway from washing away. He also did all the smaller jobs like installing a utility sink and the glass door that separated the kitchen from the rest of the house. This door kept the peace between the cats at night. He was very handy. I have so many good memories.

As a widow, I kept myself exhaustively busy, so I never had time to examine my thoughts and feelings. Busyness was a wonderful distraction. Buying a new house and moving seemed like a wonderful new project. I enjoyed projects, but was the new house merely a way to keep myself from dealing with my feelings for another year?

When I became aware of what I was doing to myself, I slowed down and did some interior listening for a couple of weeks. Sometimes I sat in my red leather recliner to meditate, other times I sat up tall on a formal oak chair in my dining room. Wherever I sat, as I stilled my body and mind, I found a jumble of conflicting thoughts that seemed to change from day to day, sometimes hour to hour. The current motivators in my life seemed to be fear of the unknown and the desire to protect myself. This made sense since I had no idea what the rest of my life would bring. And being cautious at this vulnerable time was a good idea. I decided to accept these feelings and give myself more time to heal.

Sitting still is difficult for me. I like to be moving, doing. There is another way of finding clarity that works better for me than meditating. I watch myself. I listen to myself talk to other people. Often, I am surprised by what I hear myself say, and I realize that I had the answer all the time. I just needed to verbalize it.

I looked at houses the whole time I argued with myself about staying or moving. I told myself it was part of the process to decide if I really wanted to move. I knew I wanted something smaller than what I had. Something with a compact yard that came with a landscape contract. Something I could manage by myself. I looked at houses in the village, but many of them had long floor plans like mine in the woods. I made an offer on a house there but didn't get it.

In the course of a couple of months, I bought the fifth house I saw. It was a mile away from my current home. It was in the same village, so I could keep my friends and activities with no need to find new doctors, new grocery stores, or new travel routes. This felt like the right thing to do. If I had to be single, I wanted a different house to embody my new life. I wanted to retain the memories of our first house, but to move on to create a new life alone.

the move

John and I cleaned out twenty-five years of relics when we moved to North Carolina, but downsizing now was particularly challenging; I couldn't keep it all. My current move was an excellent opportunity to take an incremental step towards making the transition to a retirement community later. I had been to enough estate sales to see the possessions people needed to unload when they moved to a small apartment. The change from large house with years of belongings to apartment with the bare minimum seemed like a shock to the system. My downsizing now would make future scaling back easier.

I am a natural organizer and love sorting through things. I enjoyed seeing what forgotten treasures closets held deep in their dark corners. I relished reviewing my possessions, pondering their value to my life, and making decisions about whether to sell, donate, or keep each piece. Was this item practical? Did I use it? If I didn't use it and it wasn't practical, did I have an emotional attachment to it? All of these were reasons to keep an item. When my daughter visited, we culled my wardrobe. I tried on all my clothes—an impromptu fashion show—and she passed judgment. This sweater was too long, that color didn't do anything for me, those pants were too baggy. I did, however, keep the pants she referred to as "mom" pants.

Unfortunately, not all of the things I sorted through were mine; many were John's. How could I give his things away? Didn't I want to hold them dear? In the end, I decided that I couldn't carry his possessions with me for the rest of my life. They didn't hold the same meaning for me that they did for him. I remember him lying in bed and asking me, "Who will continue my stamp collection when I die?" I didn't know what to say. He had a wonderful collection that he started as a child, but I didn't enjoy collecting stamps. Neither Henry nor Grace were interested. I eventually sold it to the company from whom he had bought so many of his stamps. While he was sick, he and I sold or gave away his erector set, telescope, and toy rockets, but he had kept a wooden fort replete with soldiers and Indians that was the last gift his father had given him after leaving the family when John was three. This held great sentimental value for him, but not for me. This was not something we would want to pass on to grandchildren. Who wanted to tell them the story about United States soldiers stealing Indian land?

In addition to John's pastimes, he brought furniture into the marriage. He was an avid reader and bought two barris-ter's bookcases. We sold one before he died, and I sold the other after I had given away most of his books. The question of his oak desk remained. I had refinished it after his death. This was the desk he referred to when he said he was going to come back as a desk while talking to Grace and me. How could I part with it? Finally, I reasoned that if he was coming back it wouldn't be as that desk. Both the bookcase and desk sold quickly for hefty sums. At least I showed respect.

I gave the ladies who cleaned my house some hand-thrown pottery. One beautiful soup tureen with a clay ladle was a wedding gift. It had never been practical and sat on the shelf for thirty-five years as an ornament. The other piece was an exquisite teapot with a delicate horizontal ridge pattern running around the entirety of the pot. This had been a gift from John's old girlfriend, who had been a source of tension when we started dating. Making sure I didn't break it had always been a running joke between us. It had a matching honey pot. I never used honey.

My own childhood toys held other dilemmas. My father had made a two-foot-long mahogany doll crib with a side rail that moved up and down like a real crib. He also made a matching wardrobe for doll clothes and a doll highchair. I had kept these pieces for sixty-five years and planned to pass them on to my grandchildren. I had a dollhouse I bought with my own money when I was small. My father taught me to save at a very young age, so I bought a Poor Pitiful Pearl doll and Steiff stuffed animals that I still have. There were wooden puzzles that my brother and I played with. Since neither of my children was married, time was running out for passing these treasures on.

I sold each wooden puzzle on eBay, making frequent trips to the post office to mail them. I sold the dollhouse and many smaller items to an antique store in a neighboring town, but the owner wasn't interested in the wooden doll furniture my dad had made. I eventually donated it and other unsold items to a thrift store. It was wrenching to sort through my own past and throw out entire chunks of my life.

As challenging as downsizing was, there was still packing to do. When John's company moved us to North Carolina, it paid to pack us. Now that I was paying, I decided to pack myself. I was certainly capable of wrapping things in paper and putting them in boxes. I just couldn't move the boxes once they were filled. True to form, I got an early start and lived amid boxes for about a month.

A week before I moved, I frequently drove to the new house to oversee workmen who were hanging a storm door, changing locks, laying hardwood floors, and installing granite in the bathrooms. A plumber needed to come the day before and the day after the granite was placed. Despite my seeming efficiency, I was still putting things in boxes when the movers arrived.

new house, new life

Buying a new house was an act of rebellion. I wanted to be free from the tyranny of reminders that John was not there and that I was living in our house alone. Every day that I opened our post office box and found mail for him, I groaned. It reminded me of his death. In my most unforgiving moments, I accused myself of running away, not that this is always a bad option. In my best moments, I saw my move as a positive step towards creating a new life, embracing my new single self, and having something that was all mine, a true expression of my personality.

My new home had a spacious feel, although it was smaller than my previous one. The fourteen-foot living room ceiling was banked with windows that filled the room with light and looked out on a backdrop of trees. The kitchen was a strip of counter at the end of this large room. A screened porch, den, dining room, and three bedrooms surrounded this hub. Every room was painted a sunny yellow. I was delighted with the warmth and cozy arrangement. There was hardly any yard and a very short driveway. What's more, it was in move-in condition. I only needed to remove the carpet and replace it with hardwood because of my dust and pet hair allergies. And since I had remodeled the bathrooms in my last house a year and a half earlier, I planned to add granite counters to these bathrooms as well.

Before buying, I had carefully analyzed the space to figure which pieces of my furniture would fit. I measured rooms and furniture to make an accurate floor plan of the new space. John and I had collected most of our antique furniture over thirty-six years of marriage. Every piece had a story. I had refinished most of them and didn't want to part with any of it. I was nervous about moving to a smaller space because I had filled four utility room closets, a coat closet, a linen closet, a bedroom closet, and two walk-in closets in my old house. The new one had two bedroom closets, a coat closet, and one walk-in closet, four in all versus nine in the old one. Even after careful planning and culling through possessions, I still brought some extra furniture to give myself options.

Grace came from Boston to help me move. It never occurred to me how necessary it was to have two people on the day of a move. Grace watched the cats on the screen porch at the old house and bought lunch for the crew while I answered questions, went to the new house to show the movers where to put the furniture, and sat down with the crew leader to go over paperwork and write a check.

After the movers left the new house, Grace and I tried some furniture arrangements in the living room. Friends Peg and Jim dropped by to pick up my empty boxes for their own move, so we moved the furniture again with Peg's help. The rest of the furniture fell into place easily: beds and bureaus in bedrooms and my desk and most of my boxed supplies in my office. Within a week's time almost everything was in place, and I hosted my women's spirituality group. They were amazed that I organized everything so fast. My motivation was my inability to tolerate things out of place. For the rest of the summer, I continued to tweak cabinet knobs, faucets, and showerheads, but by September I was fully settled. My new life had begun.

Was I free of thinking of John now that I was in a new space? No, not at all. What I failed to calculate was that my fondest memories were of John and me doing home projects. He had a lot of know-how, and I loved learning new carpentry tricks from him. We worked well as a team—he built and I painted or refinished. Whenever we finished a project, we stood back to admire our work and said, "It looks like it was always meant to be this way."

In the new house, every time I fixed or adjusted something, I thought of John. I was grateful for all the things he had taught me—the right-hand rule for figuring out which way to unscrew something, how to stick a toothpick into a screw hole to tighten it up when the screw was too small, how to shim a hinge, how to remove the trap from the sink. Every time I had to call a handyman because I couldn't do something myself, I thought of John and how he could have done this task. John replaced disposals, fixed toilets, unclogged sinks. He did electrical work, climbed on roofs, re-tarred flashing, and cleaned out gutters. Now I was dependent on other men, men I happily paid to do things for me.

I also was happy to pay a real estate agent's fee when I was looking for a house and later to sell my old one. I didn't want to buy or sell a house without some emotional support. As I looked at houses and pondered making an offer on one, I wanted someone to talk it over with and to weigh the pros and cons, just as I would have done with John. The agent I chose was perfect for me. He had construction knowledge and could talk about the cost to fix rotting exterior trim or where to install a cat door. He sold me my new house and then sold my house in the woods. With all the advice and support he offered, I began to think of him as a rent-a-husband.

When my father died, I took some of his small tools. When John died, I was left with hand tools, power tools, bicycle tools, discarded hospital tools, and tools I can't describe. Even though John was terrific about helping me sort through the boxes of plumbing and electrical supplies before he died, I still had a lot of tools. He had also written copy to advertise his Shopsmith, a versatile woodworking machine, that I was able to sell soon after his death.

After we finished going through the garage, John announced, "Okay, I think we need to teach you how to use power tools now." I was horrified. I had no intention of using power tools on my own. I thought this was so funny I mentioned his quip to his cousin Faye. She said, "Oh, yes, I have a circular saw and electric hedge trimmers." I let the topic drop and donated the circular saw and hedge clippers along with some of the other scary power tools to the Habitat ReStore. I kept the electric drill.

In summer 2019, after I moved, I finally took the time to sort through and reorganize the tools. I had been dreading this task. There were so many tools, many duplicates, and so many I didn't know what to do with. I put the ones I didn't recognize in boxes and dropped them off at the Habitat ReStore. The others I organized into multiple toolboxes. Who needs more than one toolbox? I have a box for hammers—a tack hammer, a ball peen hammer (not sure what to do with this), a couple of large claw hammers, a small claw hammer, and a rubber mallet. I have a box of different-sized pliers and wire cutters. I have a small drawer full of hemostats that John collected from a hospital's discards. These are good for removing bits of paper stuck in my paper shredder.

Cleaning out the garage was my last task before feeling fully organized. After cleaning it out and settling in, I was starting to accept my life as a single woman. I felt at home.

impatience

I was impatient for grief to be over. I wanted to move on. It's not that I wasn't trying. I had attended two different bereavement groups, seen two therapists, stayed active with volunteer activities, regularly got together with friends, and moved to a new house. What more could I have done? I could have waited patiently and put more time behind me. Like a child's plaintive, "Are we there yet?" I had to accept that it took time to get there. And some people take longer than others, particularly people who try to push down their grief, as I did.

When I worked in Boston, I was exasperated by waiting, particularly in standstill traffic. Sometimes I felt so pressed to get things done that I filled my wasted time with little tasks. I clipped and filed my fingernails and even did my toenails a couple of times as I sat stalled on the highway.

I learned to appreciate waiting when we were house hunting. I wanted to check out the neighborhood of a house John and I were interested in. I sat in my car for a half hour. Nothing happened at first. Then a delivery truck drove up. Some kids walked by. I watched a man jump in his car and drive off in a hurry. Hmmm.

As I aged, I enjoyed being forced to pause. Waiting was an opportunity to look around and see things I'd be too busy to notice otherwise. Stopped in traffic, I looked at cars, I looked at drivers. What were they doing? In an elevator, I observed the décor. What did I think of it? In the doctor's waiting room, I wondered who these people were. Were they seeing my doctor? What was the staff like?

There is a freedom in waiting. My grief-motivated busy-ness had me trapped. I needed a change in attitude, to look around, smell the air, and listen to my grief. My desire to move through my bereavement quickly was holding me back from moving through my sadness. I have heard different descriptions of this phenomenon. My therapist described it as being chased by a monster who eventually catches up. Of course, when it catches up you will have to deal with it.

I won a prize at the local garden club when I was twelve for growing a robust impatiens plant. Impatiens is a flowering, shade-loving plant. In the sun, its stems can look barren, and it needs to be watered more often. Its natural habitat is a shady, moist environment where it rewards you with beautiful thick, red, pink, and magenta blooms. I have grown impatiens for almost sixty years and now see that caring for them is similar to dealing with grief. If I try to hurry my grief along by maintaining a sunny disposition, I will struggle and need more care. If I acknowledge the dark days and let my grief take its own course, I will be rewarded with the peace I seek.

widowhood

Soon after John died, I asked my friend Beth, "Do people mind when I talk about him?"

She looked at me incredulously, coffee cup suspended halfway to her mouth. She put the cup down. "Not only do we mind, but it reminds us that it could happen to our husbands."

The mood of our cozy lunch date suddenly changed. I stared out of the café window. I thought, there is no way I am going to stop talking about John.

Making the switch from thinking in terms of being a couple to thinking in terms of the singular me was a long process. If I talked about a trip John and I took to Tanzania, I felt like I was misrepresenting the situation if I used the first person singular. I didn't go alone. John and I went together. As time went on and I did more and more things by myself—took a train trip to Washington, DC, for Thanksgiving or drove to

Boston for the summer—it was easier to talk about what I did by myself. But it still felt strange not to speak as if I was coupled.

During the first year of bereavement, I signed up for a group trip to museums in a nearby city thinking this would be a good diversion. The well-meaning coordinator said, "We have a few other single ladies on the trip." I thought, Single lady? I am no single lady. I am a widow!

I was incensed. She was stripping me of my identity. During lunch with Beth, I mentioned this exchange. She said, "Well, single lady has a more positive ring to it than widow." She was right, but it undercut the experience of my grief and transition.

The word *widow* connotes loss, but it also indicates status. There are privileges associated with marriage and benefits to being coupled. In an altercation outside the marriage, married people have someone to back them up. They pay lower taxes, can inherit tax-free from their spouse, or can visit their partner in the hospital with no questions asked. And there are emotional benefits that enhance health and prolong life. Couples have something of value—a life partner, a legitimacy. I had lost all of that.

John and I treasured being married. We both had experienced loneliness in our twenties. At some point in each of our young lives, we each had eaten Thanksgiving dinner alone in a restaurant far from home. We both shuddered to remember those awkward and sad restaurant experiences, something we hoped to never experience again. We were so grateful to have found each other, to have found love, companionship, and the opportunity to start a family. We loved doing house-hold projects together, solving problems, creating a beautiful home. We actively maintained our relationship and never used harsh words with each other. During a phone conversation, a friend overheard me speaking to John and commented, "You are so polite to your husband."

We enjoyed spending time together. Once we met a neighbor in the grocery store who said, "Oh, that's so cute. You're shopping together." We made most major decisions together. And we were secure enough to include single friends in our social circle. When we married, we vowed never to abandon our unmarried friends. Many married people cling to other couples or shun uncoupled friends who may have lost partners through death, divorce, or illness, or maybe never had a partner.

On another lunch date, I asked my spunky septuagenarian friend Janet, "What are your thoughts about being a widow?"

"What do you mean?" she said. "I talk to Tom all the time. We were married for forty years. When I have to fill out one of those forms where they ask me to check a box—married, single, widowed—I check married. It is none of their business. Anyway, it is for privacy. I don't know who has access to that form." And I suspect because, in her mind, she is still married to Tom and always will be.

Another friend writes letters to her deceased husband sharing news of his family members, friends, and colleagues. This keeps her connected through the memories of sights, sounds, and feelings. These women keep their relationships with their husbands alive. Maintaining a day-to-day relationship with John never occurred to me. In fact, I resisted it. I kept hoping to move on to another relationship.

At some point after John's death, I had the thought that relationships exist only in our minds. There are day-to-day interactions, kindnesses that make us feel cherished, and satisfying physical contact, but relationships are not tangible. They are conjured from our thoughts and feelings. We choose what we take in or what we remember. What about the people who are fooled into thinking that their partner is faithful? Or a woman married to a man who leads a double life with two families? We all create our own narratives that make us happy or not so happy. It makes some sense to continue a relationship with a spouse whose body has left this world.

While in the airport waiting to return to North Carolina from Boston, I noticed a woman who appeared to be alone. Every time I returned from getting water or a snack, the woman had moved to another seat. I had to keep changing seats also, because every time I got up, my seat would be taken. The third time I moved, I sat a couple of seats away from her. We had similar bags for our sleep apnea machines, so I struck up a conversation.

"I see we have the same CPAP bag. I just started therapy in July. I expected to feel terrific after starting, but I don't. I was hoping to feel like superwoman. The only thing that is better is that I don't fall asleep while driving."

"I didn't have a dramatic recovery from sleep apnea either. I think it is because we are old," she said.

Through conversation, we revealed that we were both widows, she for twenty years, me for three. "Oh! You're a newbie!" she said.

She talked about missing her best friend—her husband—and coping with loneliness. I was surprised she admitted to being lonely. I turned the subject to dating and confided that I recently signed up for match.com. It didn't sound like she had pursued dating, but she had opinions about other people's mating dances at her bridge club.

"If you are interested in dating someone, you need to be ready to move on it. Otherwise, the casserole brigade will snap him up. I think any man who is still single at this age is probably damaged. Don't you?" Yikes, I thought. Am I damaged, too, because I am single?

Some people seek new partnerships after a loss. Others seem content to remain alone. One friend told me that her late husband was so terrific that she hasn't bothered to look for anyone else. She is sure no one could measure up. She lives happily in the large house they built out in the country.

"It gets better with time" is advice the bereaved often hear. What exactly is "it"? The sadness, the loneliness, the horror, the frustration? It is probably different for each person. After three years, the initial anguish of widowhood faded for me, and I sometimes forgot to be sensitive to the needs of newly widowed people.

While we were chatting, a recent widow mentioned a medical procedure she had endured, and I said that John had undergone a similar treatment. I saw pain flash across her face. I thought, I guess I shouldn't have said that. Maybe she associated John's death with the treatment. Or maybe the mention of my deceased husband reminded her of her own loss. We all process our grief differently, so it is difficult to know what to say or what not to say. And we all grieve different things.

I would not choose the fate of being alone. It reminds me of my initial resistance to the idea of retiring. When John broached the idea of retiring, I reacted strongly. "What?! Retire? That's the end of life. After retirement you die. I don't want to retire." John enjoyed being relaxed and looked forward to taking it easy. Not me. I enjoy being busy. In the end, we handled retirement in our own ways. He retired, stayed home, and did some volunteer work. I took a job as a freelance video producer so I could slow down gradually. When I was completely retired, I packed my days with volunteer obligations.

John and I were married for thirty-six years, more than half my life at the time of this writing. My therapist said that I will always be married to John. This idea pains me. Yes, he is in my head and I talk about him and sometimes to him, but I want to leave the pain behind to find new joys. I admit, I have found new joys. They just aren't the ones I was expecting.

perks of widowhood

One of the first things I enjoyed as a widow was my new-found freedom. I saw a myriad of possibilities with my new perspective. Lest I give the wrong impression, John was not controlling or overbearing. If there were things I didn't do in my marriage, the restraint came from me. I wanted to join the concert series in our village, but he didn't, so I dropped the subject. It never occurred to me to attend alone or to find a friend to go with me. I was in a marriage with some-one whose company I enjoyed, and I wanted to share activ-ities with him. What's more, I valued our middle ground, our compromises. I had learned from collaborating with my graphic design clients that we produced a better product when there was give and take. John and I were both brought up to be independent, but we did most things together, from grocery shopping to attending the theater. I had no bevy of girlfriends with whom to hang out, no Ya-Ya Sisters to travel with. I was baffled by my friends who traveled without their husbands. I never understood why John thought I was a loyal person, but in retrospect, I get it.

In a chat with two friends, one divorced and the other widowed, they talked about how nice it was to wake up and go to bed when they wanted and to do what they wanted on their own schedule. I wholeheartedly agreed. Despite the disconcerting silence of living alone, it seemed like a privilege to break the quiet each morning. There was power in thinking that the day didn't start until I did. I only had to contend with a self-imposed schedule or a demanding, hungry cat.

All the renovation projects I took on in my old and new homes were easier because I made all the design decisions myself. I was able to get rid of many more possessions when I moved than if John had been alive, despite sometimes feeling guilty about shedding things that had held meaning for us as a couple. I know couples that rented storage units when they downsized to smaller homes because one of them wanted to keep more than the new space could accommodate.

Early in our marriage, we bought an adjustable double bed that vibrated and allowed us to raise the head or feet. At the time, we didn't want to pay for the additional six inches of width a queen-sized bed offered. We made good use of our bed by using the control to raise ourselves up and watch cartoons in bed every Saturday morning.

We had that same full-sized bed thirty years later when my legs started to bother me. I found comfort by sleeping with my legs at a right angle to my body. Unfortunately, there was not enough room for me to do this when John was in bed. As soon as he got up at five a.m., my legs snapped over to his side of the bed. After his death, I was grateful to have the entire bed to myself all night.

Looking back, I can see that holding my grief in for the first nine months created a host of physical ailments. These complaints were certainly not one of the perks of widowhood, but the privacy my aloneness afforded was welcome. When I developed acid indigestion, the doctor suggested I take a proton pump inhibitor. When I balked at taking another pill and expressed concern about some of the risks I had read about PPIs, the doctor suggested I raise the head of my bed. I opted for this. I wouldn't have been able to do this if John had been sharing the bed with me.

There were many other times when I was glad to be alone. I have trouble putting myself to sleep at night and usually rely on listening to a lecture or documentary on my iPad. When John was alive, I used ear buds, so the sound did not disturb him, but he often woke up and complained about the light from the iPad. I would sigh and turn it off and hope to fall asleep soon. After he died, I had the freedom to lie in bed for hours listening to my iPad or fall asleep listening to a favorite television show by using the set's sleep timer.

Like many people my age, I had sleep problems. I woke up as many as seven times a night. A sleep psychiatrist was sure I had sleep apnea. After three sleep studies, she had me convinced and prescribed a CPAP (Continuous Positive Airway Pressure) machine. I was horrified that life was not getting simpler, but more complicated with new hardware to manage. I remembered sleeping in a room with a friend with a CPAP machine and finding the experience Darth Vader-esque as I listened to the air being forced into his lungs. I wasn't happy about my new development, but grateful that I could sleep alone with my CPAP equipment. I didn't feel very attractive with my new face mask and tubing hooked up to a machine.

Three years into my bereavement, I developed digestive issues. I spent a lot of time in the bathroom and used rolls and rolls of toilet paper. At one time during his life, John mentioned that he thought that bowel incontinence was disgusting. I often wondered as I nursed him how he could tolerate me wiping his bottom when he had reached the point of wearing diapers. Despite his hospital experience, he was never comfortable talking about bodily fluids. Grace and I could talk openly about such things, but we were never joined by John or Henry. Clearly the specter of death had changed John's thinking, but I still wondered if our places had been reversed, would he have been able to do some of the yuckier nursing duties for me.

I discovered being by myself allowed me to be more engaged with my environment. I had a new perspective on what I looked at. If I was in a restaurant with John, or anyone, I would be paying attention to them, not looking around the establishment. Sitting alone, I noticed décor, interesting objects on the walls, other diners, and the piped-in music.

When I went to Washington, DC, to spend Thanksgiving visiting museums by myself a few months after John died, I enjoyed viewing exhibits at my own pace, not feeling obligated to connect with a companion by saying something like,

"Oh, did you see this?" or "I'm going to the gift shop now." Grace has always complained that I spend too much time reading every word in an exhibit. By myself, I spent as much time as I wanted and chatted up strangers during lunch in the museum cafes.

I was a busy working woman when I lived in Boston, never slowing down long enough to take in the details of my surroundings. When I visited a couple of years after John's death, I was surprised that I saw things I had never noticed before. As a semi-tourist, I stopped in plazas and took the time to visit the refurbished Boston Public Library. They had added two eateries, so I sat in their gorgeous courtyard and shared my lunch table with a couple from out of town. The square pale-blue pool in the center of the courtyard shimmered as a hundred tiny jets of water arced onto its surface. A bronze statue rose from its core. People sat staring at the water, in pairs and triplets, but one young man's pensive gaze stopped me. There was a faraway quality to his reverie—boyfriend or girlfriend trouble, contemplating a change in college major, a bad job situation, should he abandon his PhD?

His sadness reminded me of my own. What expression did I have on my face? I caught a glimpse of my reflection in a window the day before and was horrified at the lines pulling my mouth downward. Was it the drier climate in Boston and the fact I had forgotten to bring my favorite moisturizer? Or was it that the loss of my husband had finally caught up with me and my carefully crafted reserve was showing cracks? I reminded myself to smile.

John and I had long enjoyed Arts and Crafts Mission-style furniture. For my birthday, I treated myself to the annual Arts and Crafts Conference at Asheville's venerable Grove Park Inn. I had some lovely, expensive, lonely meals. It struck me that this may be living, but it didn't seem like life without someone to share it with.

The novelty of going places by myself wore off after a couple of years. I allowed myself prudent luxuries like using valet parking. But this was really a safety measure, so I didn't walk down long, dark streets to where my car was parked. Even these perks lost their charm. I was sick of being by myself.

I am aware that many of the things I have identified as perks are rationalizations. Of course, I would rather have had John in the picture. We would have worked out the challenges of getting older. However, I like to look on the bright side. Putting a positive spin on as many aspects of my new life as possible has made my loss more bearable.

triggers

Grief can strike at the most surprising times. The reminders of John were everywhere. If I saw an older couple enjoying each other's company, I yearned for John. If I heard big band music, I thought of John. Music has always had a way of reaching me emotionally. There were certain songs that we sang in the village chorus that choked me up. Sometimes I had to mouth the words because my throat was so tight no sound came out.

A month after John died, I took my wedding ring to a jeweler to have the gold polished. We had designed our rings to have slabs of amethyst, our shared birthstone, inserted in the flat top of the wide gold bands. Amethyst is a soft stone that breaks easily, so after years of having the stones replaced, we chose a slightly harder stone, lapis lazuli. When I picked up my newly buffed ring, I was dismayed. The gold was polished, but the jeweler had cut a triangular piece out of the face of the ring. He said he had run into a flaw in the gold while buffing and had cut out the bad part.

I was flabbergasted that they hadn't called to let me know about the problem. Did they think I wouldn't notice? With tears in my eyes and the pitch of my voice rising, I communicated that this was my wedding ring and my husband had died recently. They agreed to fix it and to not charge me.

A year later, I decided to take my ring off my left hand and put it on my right as a symbol of moving on. Or was it just the hope that I was moving on? The ring was too small to fit over my enlarged knuckles on my right hand, so I spent a few days not wearing any ring, but that didn't feel right. I took the ring to a different jeweler and had it resized for my right hand. I loved that ring with its bright blue stone, but it was heavy and kept twirling around on the base of my finger. I wore it for another year, then placed it in my jewelry box with John's.

Our rings were wonderful symbols of our union. We designed them together, chose the stones together, and kept repairing them or upgrading the stones as needed, similar to a marriage.

Two months after John died, I decided to make space in the garage by donating his bike. Giving it up was huge in my mind. His bicycle was iconic. After spending two years in Oklahoma City working as a conscientious objector to the Vietnam War in his twenties, John spent the winter in Minnesota with his sister Peggy and her family. He made a sleeping bag and bike panniers from kits using her treadle sewing machine.

When spring arrived, he took off on his bike across the west, heading for California, camping and working on farms as he went. This was one of the highlights of his life that he referred to frequently when we first met. He knew everything about bikes. I gave up his bike but kept his bike tools.

I asked the local thrift shop to pick up his bicycle. I left it in front of my garage with a note attached when I left the house for appointments and errands. Hours later when I returned, I saw the thrift store truck in my driveway, so I waited in my car on the street until they had left. I watched two men lift the bike into the back of the truck and drive off. It seemed surreal. I cried. They took a piece of me that day.

I felt heartsick when I sorted through John's email account to save meaningful emails. Then, with some trepidation, I deleted it. His account was no longer attracting messages that defined his life. It was choked with junk mail. He was better than that. In my mind he was a vibrant personality, not a languishing email account used only for promotional email and scams. I chose what I wanted to remember and what I was willing to let go.

I had occasional bouts of sadness borne out of my loneliness, but nothing very demonstrative. At dinner time or while I did my physical therapy exercises, I had a habit of watching *Law and Order: Special Victims Unit* on television. I had been watching this show religiously since John died. There was something soothing about the familiar mix of detective work and legal wrangling that kept me hooked. I also suspected that the characters were so familiar to me that I saw them as reliable friends. When the four of us traveled as a family and stayed in a hotel room, *Law and Order* was the only TV show we could all agree to watch as we sat lined up in our two double beds at night. The show reminded me of those family times.

One evening as I hoisted my arms above my head holding my five-pound weights, a commercial aired advertising a drug for women with metastatic breast cancer. Images of a woman settling her son into his college dorm room flowed across the screen. I suddenly started sobbing. I rarely sobbed, but the suggestion that people with metastatic cancer could go on with their normal lives was in stark contrast with my experience. Who had the energy to do anything when they had metastatic cancer? John certainly didn't. He was so sick and miserable that all he could do was take naps and occasionally work at his desk to pay a bill or two. These ads made me mad. Was this false advertising? The actors all looked so healthy.

Eventually I realized I knew people who had metastatic cancer, and they were up walking around. In fact, they looked great. I had friends who had survived. One friend had been disease-free for two years after having stage-four cancer. Why was John's case so different? Why was he so sick? Why wasn't there a cure for his cancer? The thought of the pain caused by his illness and treatment is still gut-wrenching for me.

When I tried to leave behind the reminders of my past life by moving to a new house, to minimize anything that exposed my sadness, I found that triggers remained. I no longer received mail addressed to John, but during that summer and fall, PBS ran specials commemorating the fiftieth anniversary of the Apollo 11 moon landing. John was fascinated by space and even had a telescope when he was a child. He would have loved this, I thought every time I saw one of the promotions.

As I let go of the places, experiences, and things that reminded me of John, I harbored a small fear that some future day I might regret not having them—particularly his computer or back-up hard drive that I erased. Each time I let go of a piece of computer equipment, I reminded myself that it would soon become outdated. These objects should go to someone who could use them, not sit in my dark closet. The most important things were the memories I tucked away in my mind. I can always pull them out in a safe, private moment or wait until the next time they make surprise appearances.

where we are now

A few years after we started the dinner group from my bereavement program, we had a reunion. Charlie, the retired pastor and oldest member of our group, called our little band the Good Grief Group and reserved a room at a local restaurant, where about twenty of us gathered. Some members still attended the drop-in bereavement meetings, but I had stopped going. I didn't feel the need for weekly support, but still enjoyed the socializing. Some, like me, had been part of the group for three or more years, some for much less.

Since we had been part of the group at different times, Charlie had us introduce ourselves and give a little update. One person said she was glad to see how happy and relaxed we all looked now that we had gone through the worst part of our grief. I thought to myself, I'm not over this!

We were all in very different emotional places. My friend Tad attended with his new wife Mary. Two other attendees who married after meeting in the group were there as well. The man had had a knee replacement a week earlier. His wife told the group that on the second night of their marriage, he collapsed unconscious in the bathroom twice. Then he had a cancer scare, but surgery showed the tumor was benign. Not an ideal way to start a marriage, but older adults need to be ready for anything.

Coupling seemed to be a natural inclination. Many of us who weren't coupled had looked for or were still looking for companions. My friend, Janet, who still talks to her late husband daily, doesn't seem to be interested in pursuing another partner. She is more interested in staying out of the hospital, having had some bad falls, one down twenty-four steps.

One group member said, "I've met three wonderful women online, but they were all in towns too far away for convenient dating. Now I have a relationship with a four-legged companion that sticks to me like Velcro." After his wife died, he cleaned out a 2,600-square-foot home and moved to what he called a more appropriately sized home—1,200 square feet.

A woman who was planning to sell her house eventually said she took twenty-four boxes of paper to a shredding event. She had more sorting to do—piles of things to keep, things to give away, and things for her children. A man she had met in another bereavement group sat next to her.

Two attendees had moved to continuing care retirement communities. One of them, a man who had confided to me months earlier that he planned to move into the CCRC, meet someone, and remarry had found a partner within months and moved into her home. He said that he and his partner spent a lot of time taking each other to medical appointments.

The other, who had outlived two husbands and a boyfriend, chose a retirement facility she used to work at as a teenager. She had been living there contentedly for about a year but found she had brought too much and was still sorting through boxes. She was thankful she had a guest room for the overflow and a second bathroom where she stored more items in the bathtub.

Clearly, we do not need to forget the past to create a new life. I used to see forgetting the past as the only choice. Most people I have talked to about living with loss keep their loved one alive within the context of their new relationship. One widowed friend told me that when she told her long-term, long-distance boyfriend that she wouldn't be upset if he dated other women, he replied, "Well, I am still very attached to Barbara." My friend replied, "And I am still very attached to my Jerry."

Another widower told me that he keeps a picture of his late wife next to his bed. When he comes home after a date, he says good night to his late wife before he climbs into bed.

And me? I remain busy and single, living with two elderly cats. Occasionally, I have lunch or dinner with Charlie or Tad.

death is all around

John had been gone for three years, three months, and thirteen days when I sat down to write this chapter. I felt well adjusted, well on my way to being healed. Yet an awareness of death permeated my daily life. Our culture doesn't like to talk about death, but the reality is that many of us have been touched by it and eventually will have to confront our own deaths. I still find value in bereavement groups and activities, because they are frequented by people who have walked the same solitary path I have. Feelings get trapped inside and need to be released. Talking heals. One friend likens grief to post-traumatic stress syndrome. We are subject to triggers because we have a heightened awareness of death while the rest of our culture looks the other way.

When I have free time, I move the pictures from my iPad to an organized set of folders in the cloud. I leave a few of my favorites on the iPad, the way I used to carry family pictures in my wallet. The last pictures I have of John were taken right before he went into hospice care. He was painfully thin and was trying gamely to smile. Some might think that this is the last way I would want to remember him in his wasted body, but these pictures are precious to me.

John's sister objected to the image I chose for the final page of his memorial photo book, a picture of John wearing a face mask to measure his oxygen while riding an exercise bike for a patient study. This was John, bravely carrying on, contributing to something bigger than himself. I was proud that he chose to participate in multiple studies while he was ill. This is why I love these pictures.

Not too long ago, I received an email saying that one of my neighbors had died of brain cancer. I had never met him or his wife, even though they lived one street over from me. A couple of neighbors had mentioned them to me from time to time.

"Bob has brain cancer, but he has lived much longer than doctors expected." And, "I used to see Ginny and Bob out walking together, but Ginny said he doesn't have the strength to do that anymore."

When I read the email saying he had died, my first instinct was to knock on the widow's door, introduce myself, and tell her that I was a widow also. Like her, I knew grief. Welcome to the club.

On second thought, I decided that was too presumptuous. I had no right to pierce her privacy. I tried to put myself in her shoes. What would I have thought if a stranger knocked on my door a day or two after John's death, professing sympathy? I think I would have received it with gratitude, unless it was the neighbor who lectured me for thirty minutes about how prayer could change my life.

It didn't matter how I would have reacted. I didn't know what this woman needed. She probably needed time to take care of funeral arrangements and to pull herself together.

I could send a card. Everyone likes getting cards. But a card from a stranger? Who was I doing this for—her or me? Everyone's grief triggers my grief, but also my compassion. Any grief story sets me thinking about my own loss. No, I will not send a card. This woman's grief is not my business. I don't even live on her street. It would be different if she lived next door, or two doors down, but that one street over puts her off limits.

I reached out to a widowed acquaintance a year or so ago. I had had business dealings with her husband and liked him. When I heard her husband had died, I emailed her, reminding her who I was and that she had attended an event at my house. I told her I was a recent widow also and she could call me to chat if she wanted to. I never heard from her. I didn't expect to. Months later, I saw her leaving the gym. I stopped her on the sidewalk.

"Hi Sarah. I'm Linda Patterson. I emailed you when Les died. How are you doing?"

She looked at me, and I sensed she didn't have a clue as to my identity. "I'm doing okay. Getting out."

"I so admired Les. He was helpful when I was looking for contractors. I was surprised when he died. I didn't realize he was ill."

"Yes, he was ill for over a year, but didn't want people to know. He was afraid that every time he saw someone in the village, they would ask how he was doing."

"My husband felt the same way. He didn't want the neighbors to know he was sick. He didn't want to be fodder for gossip."

We chatted a little longer and said good-bye. To this day when I see her in the gym, I don't think she knows who I am. Nevertheless, I felt her pain. And I still do every time I see her.

The residents in my village are mostly retired couples. If you have a partner, it is inevitable that one of you will be left alone. On the street where I used to live, six people died in the past five years. Did the street have a curse on it since some of these people were in their sixties, or did those in their seventies and eighties just age out?

While at a fundraising dinner in the village, a fellow diner and I compared whom we knew in common. When she mentioned one of my old neighbors, I asked how she was.

"She died two weeks ago."

"What?" I gasped.

She gave me the details of my neighbor's stay in the hospital, her recovery, her subsequent accident, and finally her death in the operating room. I was stunned and briefly entertained contacting her husband, but quickly dismissed it. They had moved off the street years ago. Anyway, what would I say?

It strikes me as strange that, having gone through bereavement myself, I am no better at knowing what to say to the grief-stricken. I firmly believe that acknowledging someone's loss or pain is important. I usually rely on sending a card with an anecdote about the deceased to express what they meant to me. However, in the wake of John's death, I found one note disquieting. My friend wrote saying she would always remember John's laugh. Oh my God, I thought. I don't remember the sound of his laugh. Oh no. What does this mean? Slowly the memory has returned to me, but in those early days of grief I was panicked.

When I left the fundraising dinner, I noticed an emergency vehicle with flashing lights parked a few doors down the street. I knew what that meant.

I am not only aware of and haunted by the death around me, but of my own demise. My health is compromised—I plan to have a knee replaced; my lower back gets stiff when I get up from a chair, and I hobble along for a minute before walking normally. I am already looking forward to living in a continuing care retirement community to stave off loneliness, even though I moved into a new, smaller, more manageable house. The next move will probably be my last. Yes, I am very aware that there is an end point for all of us.

quarantine

When the COVID-19 pandemic of 2020 required us to stay inside and only venture out alone, I wondered how I would survive. I had spent the last three and a half years keeping myself frenetically busy to stave off loneliness and to block out my grief. While in quarantine, I'd miss my social network at the gym. I couldn't go to Head Start to read to children. I couldn't meet with my women's spirituality group. I couldn't visit anyone—child, parents, caretakers—associated with my guardian ad litem work. Singing was considered dangerous because it spewed too many respiration droplets into the air, so my chorus and a capella group rehearsals were out. As co-vice-president of the chorus, I couldn't meet with the board. I couldn't usher at the local repertory theater. I couldn't attend the Sunday afternoon Ethical Humanist Society meetings. I couldn't go to the village lecture series, concert series, or movie nights. I couldn't go to my art history and current events classes. I was home alone with my two cats.

Pandemics are scary, dangerous times, but during the first weeks of the stay-at-home order, my world seemed secure. I was not trying to work from home with small children underfoot nor was I a gig worker suddenly without income. True, I watched my mutual funds drop drastically in the beginning of the pandemic, but historically the market always rebounded.

As things slowed down, I enjoyed being able to catch my breath, but it was the thought of social isolation that terrified me. Would I become lonely and depressed? Nothing was further from the truth. The pandemic turned out to be an opportunity to see who I was without being so busy. I got up when I wanted, ate when I wanted, and even trained the cats to sleep in by giving them food to munch on at night. They only roused themselves when I walked into the kitchen and started rattling dishes. I learned that life still went on whether I finished my to-do list or not. My house could be messy because no one was coming inside. I was free to leave dishes in the sink or household tasks undone, totally uncharacteristic of me. I cared what other people thought, but now I didn't even wear makeup or a bra when I went to the store. I wondered who I would be when life resumed after the pandemic.

The first few weeks went surprisingly well. I refinished a side table and painted a patina on a modern-looking chair to make it blend in better with my antiques. I cleaned out the garage and reviewed the contents of a couple of closets. I watched some Netflix series and read magazines. I baked muffins and made batches of eggplant Parmesan to freeze. I thoroughly enjoyed myself. I was not lonely, nor did I obsess about John. Wow, I thought. I must have gone over a hump. I was perfectly comfortable with myself.

Some of my peers professed boredom and sent angst-filled emails. Political satire, cartoons, and cute animal pictures multiplied in my email box. Email was fine, but each day I tried to talk to another human; I did plenty of talking to cats. People were forced to think outside of the box, to be more creative, to learn new ways of keeping in touch. My daughter called twice weekly, and my son contacted me asking if I had locked myself in the house. I was touched.

I recognized this gift of time as an ideal opportunity to work on this book, to finally have a long period of time to organize my thoughts and write. Most days I walked the ten-minute round trip to my mailbox, and every week I donned gloves and a mask to grocery shop. My friends had groceries delivered, but I needed to get out and see other human beings. Before the pandemic, I rarely managed to do my physical therapy exercises twice a week. Now I had plenty of time, and there was no excuse. I took my recumbent three-wheeled bike out for a ride when traffic died down on the weekends.

Zoom meetings became prevalent and helped reduce the isolation. My meetings, classes, women's group, and Quaker meetings in Boston recast themselves for the Zoom platform. At first it felt strange to sit in Quaker worship by myself, but eventually it felt perfectly normal. We had participants from Boston, me in North Carolina, and a young Friend in Turkey. My schedule started filling up again as more and more groups used Zoom. I had plans to work on long-term projects like cleaning out files with what began as extra time, but I never seemed to get to them. If these days seemed busy, how did I manage before?

Zoom was helpful, but after four months of quarantine, my mind started working more slowly from lack of social and environmental stimulation. I talked to friends near and far on the phone, but it wasn't the same as going somewhere and having human contact. When I rode my bike on the weekends, I sometimes saw a neighbor and stopped and talked. That always lifted my spirits. The isolation was starting to get to all of us, but my married friends didn't seem to feel as isolated as I did. Zoom was a wonderful connector, but it didn't fulfill all of our needs for social contact. Some of us needed hugs. An active, dedicated member of our chorus killed herself during the pandemic, a year after her husband died. Many of the chorus speculated that the quarantine isolation contributed to her pain.

There was a foreboding sense of lost time. My trip to Japan planned for April 2020 was canceled, as was a visit to my friend Peg, who had moved to Ohio. Not being able to travel made me feel that precious years were draining away. Indeed, they were, and I wasn't likely to see my children in December either.

As the days flowed into each other, I was numbed by the isolation, but felt calm and at peace with myself. I began to wonder if I was not an extrovert at all, but really an introvert. No longer did I need busyness to distract me from memories of losing my marriage to a wonderful man who had a generous heart and a rational mind. Three and a half years of grief had strengthened me into a woman who was comfortable with herself and had proven she could get her needs met. I was free to savor memories of John, to treasure our life together, but to stay firmly rooted in the present and hopeful for the future.

integration

I planted a second sprig of a lantana bush as a memorial to John in the late spring of 2019 when I first moved into my new house. I named it John. It did well, but the second year, during the spring of the pandemic, there wasn't any trace of it. I told myself that the lantana must not have survived the winter, even though I bought the heartiest variety and the winter had been mild. The plant had died, just as John had. I needed to accept that.

In the spot where John's lantana had been, I placed two large pots of tomatoes. By mid-summer I noticed that a sprout tried to push its way past the pots. I moved them in case this was John's lantana. Sure enough, by the end of the summer, John was four feet tall and five feet wide.

The resilience of his memorial bush parallels the endurance of my memories of him, despite my earlier efforts to suppress them. I have turned some of those memories into meaningful actions. John was a well-read, generous person who left me with a list of forty charities to contribute to each year. One I had never heard of was the Project on Government Oversight, a watchdog group that investigates and exposes waste, corruption, and abuse of power in the federal government. He also supported the Southern Poverty Law Center, the Natural Resources Defense Council, and Doctors Without Borders USA along with Indian tribes, local groups, and food pantries. The newsletters from these organizations keep me informed about subjects I never would have explored. Each November, I honor his memory by continuing his generosity.

John loved the US Supreme Court and that has made me much more aware of government and politics. He carried a miniature copy of the Constitution in his wallet. He followed the supreme court decisions closely, and we toured its august building and stood in the courtroom where many landmark cases, like same-sex marriage, were argued. When I listened to the memorial service for the late Supreme Court Justice Ruth Bader Ginsberg, one of the speakers told a funny story about the deceased justice. I laughed at the humor and heard John's laugh coming from my mouth. This was not my usual laugh, it sounded distinctively like John's.

I am not the same person I was before I met him. I am not even the same person I was when he died. I have grown from thinking that I needed to leave our life together behind to understanding that the thirty-eight years we spent together have molded me and left me with rich memories and legacies. I no longer feel defensive about having acquired many of his habits and interests. I cherish them.

epilogue

When I first tackled grief, I had preconceived ideas of how it would be. In my bereavement groups, I didn't feel I was approaching it the way others were. I felt out of step. I constantly wondered if I was grieving correctly. Over the years, I have talked to other grieving people who also felt out of step, maybe because we were all taking our own approaches.

I listened to a podcast in which author Jim Rendon talked about post-traumatic growth. His book, Upside: The New Science of Post-Traumatic Growth, is based on research done at the University of North Carolina at Charlotte with widows who talked about their ordeals and the trauma of losing their husbands. They also shared how much stronger they were because of the experience. They were closer to family and friends and experienced positive changes in their lives. The suffering acted as a catalyst to change. The widows examined their lives, thought about what was important to them, and made modifications. This resonated with me. I have done the same.

On television I see medical shows depicting people dying and hear the same words I heard the night John died, "I think his breathing has changed." I feel the familiar fear grip me, and my face tenses. I watch the characters react to the death. I look on wistfully, thinking, that's not how I acted. But then I sigh and realize I grieved the only way I knew how. I have forgiven myself for any of my misconceptions about grieving. I am at peace.

I have been through the fire and come out on the other side, annealed. I have made changes: I bought a new house, made new friends, started a women's group, canceled cable, and found ways to stay abreast of current events without John taking the lead. I can live by myself and be happy. I am grateful that I have had a wonderful marriage and two delightful children. We love each other. I have a beautiful home and two cats I love dearly. Life is good. I am slowing down and not as energetic as I used to be, but I can continue to craft a meaningful life without John.

acknowledgments

I am grateful to the late Ruth Harriet Jacobs, gerontologist, sociologist, educator, poet, and author for encouraging me to write my first story thirty years ago.

I am indebted to Joyce Allen, writer and teacher, who has encouraged and mentored me since I moved to North Carolina ten years ago.

The writing group Joyce led—Barbara Brister, Karan Freimark, Janice Gebel, Marilyn Pinschmidt, Andrea Savage, Mary Stevens, and Anne Tazewell—was invaluable by critically reading my chapters, asking questions, and making suggestions.

I also want to thank my publisher Nora Esthimer for making my books come to life. When I wrote my first book, she taught me a lesson I will never forget: go deeper.

I am very grateful to editor and book designer Kelly Lojk who was incredibly easy to work with and put the polish on all the details.

A big thank you goes to Laura Brightwood, LCSW and psychotherapist, who listened and observed me as I read her every chapter. Her probing questions, gentle suggestions, and stories helped me clarify my message.

My son Henry Andrew Watterson read the book twice in development and made valuable suggestions. I am very grateful for his unique insight.

I also appreciate my daughter Grace Watterson's help in remembering the various events before and after her dad's death.

Thank you to Faye Ashley, John's cousin, for being there when John died. She showed me how to be a better nurse.

Much appreciation goes to Annie Ritter and Ann Kissel for leading a well-crafted UNC Hospice grief support group. They helped me dip my toe into the work of grief and begin to identify all I had lost.

I am grateful to writer and teacher Carol Henderson, who offered unique prompts to her writing group at UNC Hospice. Much of what I wrote during those quiet hours was included in this book.

A special thank you to my "bereavement buddy" Tad McArdle and our Growing Thru Grief dinner group who deepened my bereavement experience and offered companionship at a crucial time.

The bereavement group Growing Thru Grief had a huge impact on my development as a widow. Thank you to Bill Dahl, who coordinated a myriad of resources to provide a rich and meaningful experience to this weekly group. I am grateful to the many facilitators who gave generously of their time by sensitively guiding the discussion groups. And, I am indebted to all the participants who shared their stories and expanded my understanding of grief.

Thanks, too, to Grief Oasis, another local bereavement group that offered caring facilitators and an intimate group for sharing.

My life has been richer because of the women in my Women's Spirituality Group—Winnie Booth, Ann DiGiano, Mary Heaton, Peg Kane, Nancy Keadey, Carole Kibler, Suz Robinson, Karen Shectman, and Bonnie Sullivan. Their friendship and support buoyed me through the various stages of my grief.

I particularly want to express my appreciation for Friends from Wellesley Friends Meeting in Massachusetts. They awed and humbled me when they called, sent cards, and visited from Boston while John was sick. Thank you for embracing my family and welcoming our memorial service for John.

Peg Kane has my undying gratitude for feeding my cats, bringing me food in the hospital emergency department, sitting with me as I screamed in pain while my hand was stitched up, spending the night with me after taking me home, and driving me to the pharmacy and body shop the next day. Not every friend is so generous.

I appreciate all of my friends and relatives who have been there for me throughout this journey. Thank you for lunch and dinner invitations, phone calls, cards, visits, and other kind gestures. It made a difference.

Thank you to McIntyre's Books for their generosity to the community. The bookstore was the perfect place for a book lover's memorial service. Thank you, Pete Mock, for making my vision a reality.

I am very thankful that Tami Boardman, Paul Fehrenbach, Marlene Jones, Annie Ritter, and Karen Shectman took time out of their busy Decembers to review my manuscript and write reviews.

So many people, close friends, neighbors, acquaintances, and strangers from North Carolina to Massachusetts, and relatives from Texas to Minnesota made my path through grief a little easier and helped contribute to my experiences and the stories in this book. Thank you.

about the author

Linda Patterson grew up in a family that told stories around the dinner table. Her art talent led her into a thirty-year career in communications as a graphic designer in Boston, Massachusetts. When she took a job in direct marketing, she fell in love with writing. In 2012 she and her husband relocated to North Carolina where she put visual and verbal communications together by freelancing as a video producer for UNC-TV.

More recently Linda has turned her energies to writing from her own experience. Her first book, *What We Do for Love: Cats in the Family*, chronicled her childhood experiences with cats as she loved and lost them. As an adult, her cats were much more challenging, which inspired the book. Along the way she learned how to grieve.